Edexcel

Functional Skills
English

Written by Eileen Sagar and Keith Washington
Consultants: Jen Greatrex and Bill Kaill

Level 1

Teacher guide

A PEARSON COMPANY

Heinemann is an imprint of Pearson Education Limited,
a company incorporated in England and Wales, having its
registered office at Edinburgh Gate, Harlow, Essex, CM20 2JE.
Registered company number: 872828

www.pearsonschoolsandfecolleges.co.uk

Heinemann is a registered trademark of Pearson Education Limited

Text © Pearson Education Limited, 2010

First published 2010

British Library Cataloguing in Publication Data
A catalogue record for this book is available from the British Library.

ISBN 978 1 846 908 81 1

Copyright notice
All rights reserved. No part of this publication may be reproduced in any form or by any means (including photocopying or storing it in any medium by electronic means and whether or not transiently or incidentally to some other use of this publication) without the written permission of the copyright owner, except in accordance with the provisions of the Copyright, Designs and Patents Act 1988 or under the terms of a licence issued by the Copyright Licensing Agency, Saffron House, 6–10 Kirby Street, London EC1N 8TS (www.cla.co.uk). Applications for the copyright owner's written permission should be addressed to the publisher.

Produced by Pearson Education Ltd, 2010
Designed and produced by Kamae Design, Oxford
Original illustrations © Pearson Education, 2010
Cover design by Pete Stratton
Cover photo/illustration © Shutterstock Images
Printed in the UK by Ashford Colour Press

Acknowledgements
The author and publisher would like to thank the following individuals and organisations for permission to reproduce copyright material:

The Silly Army website text and 'Health and Safety Guidance for New Members letter' is reproduced by kind permission of The Silly Army sports club (http://www.spanglefish.com/sillyarmy); 'Work Experience – What You Need To Know' information sheet. Content provided courtesy of Oxfordshire Education Business Partnership (www.oebp.org.uk); Text from the Legoland website, reproduced by kind permission of LEGOLAND Windsor (http://www.legoland.co.uk/).

Every effort has been made to contact copyright holders of material reproduced in this book. Any omissions will be rectified in subsequent printings if notice is given to the publishers.

Websites
The websites used in this book were correct and up-to-date at the time of publication. It is essential for tutors to preview each website before using it in class so as to ensure that the URL is still accurate, relevant and appropriate. We suggest that tutors bookmark useful websites and consider enabling students to access them through the school/college intranet.

Contents

Introduction
iv

Schemes of work
Reading 1
Speaking, listening and communication 3
Writing 4

Functional Skills mapping
Key Stage 3 matching grids 6
GCSE matching grids 11
Skills checklist 16
Functional Skills English Level 1 student book at a glance 19

Lesson plans
Reading 21
Speaking, listening and communication 37
Writing 41

Assessment
How students will be assessed 53
Sample assessment materials
    Reading section 56
    Writing section 65
Sample student answers
    Reading – pass 74
    Reading – fail 80
    Writing – pass 86
    Writing – fail 92

Practice assessments
    Reading section 97
    Speaking, listening and communication section 106
    Writing section 109

Introduction

The Functional Skills English qualification is designed to give candidates the skills to operate confidently, effectively and independently in education, work and everyday life. This has been created in response to employers' perceptions that students are not achieving a sufficiently firm grounding in the basics.

About this Teacher Guide

All materials in this Teacher Guide will help you with the planning, delivery and assessment preparation of Functional Skills English. All pages are provided in both print and CD form so that you may print off the resources you require, and if you wish adapt them to your own requirements.

Schemes of work

This Teacher Guide provides schemes of work for delivering the three elements of Functional Skills English – Reading, Speaking, listening and communication and Writing – at Level 1, using the Level 1 student book. On pages 1 to 5 of this guide you will find summary schemes of work for each of the three elements, based on the content in the student book. The schemes of work are expanded in the lesson plans on pages 21 to 52.

Lesson plans and approaches to teaching

All lessons in the student book are supported by lesson plans. These give clear guidance on:
- the aims and learning objectives for the lesson
- how to introduce the lesson in a starter activity
- working through the teaching text and activities in the student book effectively
- how to draw the lesson together in a plenary
- ideas for homework.

All the activities in the lesson plans can be approached via a range of methods – individual work, pairs, small groups, pairs with an observer who feeds back, or whole class with whiteboard or posters. You should use a variety of these approaches, deciding which is most appropriate for specific classes/lessons.

The lesson plans also offer sample student answers to activities in the student book where appropriate, giving you a ready-to-use benchmark for what to expect from your students. Where activities require open student writing, no sample answers have been provided. Each section of lesson plans is introduced by an overview of how to approach teaching, with teaching ideas and guidance related to the lessons. The length of lessons will vary according to the interests and abilities of your students. You may wish to tailor the materials as you use them by using the files on the CD.

Integrating with the Key Stage 3 curriculum or with GCSE

Functional Skills English can be taught during KS3 or alongside GCSE. Customisable matching grids for both are provided on pages 6 to 15 to assist with your planning.

Assessment preparation and practice

Clear guidance on how students will be assessed is provided on pages 53 to 55. This guidance is also provided direct to the student in appropriate language within the student book (pages 112 to 114), and supplemented with *Top tips* for success. This is intended to develop students' awareness of the nature of each assessment and, equally importantly, how they need to respond in order to demonstrate functionality. For example, at Level 1, students will be expected to demonstrate that they can adapt writing forms according to purpose, respond appropriately to the specific demands of the reading questions and participate appropriately in discussions.

In addition, each section in the student book ends with a *Test zone*. Here students are given examples of the kinds of questions and tasks they will encounter in their assessments, helpfully annotated by the examiner to draw attention to what is required. Share these sections with students and have them complete the questions, drawing on the examiner's supporting comments, to embed understanding of how they will be assessed. Use the sample 'pass' and 'fail' answers, the accompanying summaries from the examiner and the self-assessment features in the student book to further develop their understanding. Draw attention to the tips from the examiner, which direct students to common errors and strategies for working effectively.

On pages 56 to 73 of this guide you will find reproduced the full text of the sample assessment materials issued by Edexcel. Use these to give your students full assessment practice. Pages 74 to 96 offer examples of students' responses to the sample assessment materials, helping you to demonstrate to students what represents a pass or fail answer. Use the examiner's commentary to expand upon what is required to gain marks.

Two further complete practice assessments are provided at the end of the student book and on pages 97 to 113 of this guide.

Schemes of work

Reading

Introduction to the scheme of work for Reading

Functional English Level 1 Reading helps students to develop a range of skills for reading, understanding and comparing texts.

The Level 1 skill standard for Reading: *read and understand a range of straightforward texts*. These skills help students to:

- identify the main points and ideas and how they are presented in a variety of texts
- read and understand texts in detail
- utilise information contained in texts
- identify suitable responses to texts.

Lesson	Aim	Learning objective	Activities	Resources
1 **Reading a range of texts**	Learn to read different types of texts.	Understand what kind of text you are reading. Find the information you need in a text.	Students review different features and forms of text and how these can be used to work out what information the text contains. They then practise by answering questions based on a range of different texts.	student book pages 8–11
2 **Working out what a text is about**	Read and understand the points and ideas in a text.	Work out what a text is about and what its purpose is.	Students work out the purpose of a text by understanding the writer's intentions.	student book pages 12–13
3 **Finding the information you need in a text**	Use different techniques to search for information in texts.	Use different ways of finding information in a text. Identify key words in a task. Find the key words in a text.	Students look for key words and scan a text to look for information in order to answer questions based on the text.	student book pages 14–15
4 **Reading closely for detailed understanding**	Read a text closely to understand texts in detail.	Use close reading to find and understand details in a text.	Students identify features and scan the text, then use close reading to gain a detailed understanding of what the text is about.	student book pages 16–17
5 **Identifying the main point in a paragraph**	Identify the main points and how they are presented in a variety of texts.	Identify the main point in a paragraph. Explain what the main ideas are in a text.	Students look at the whole text, then read a paragraph in detail to identify the main point.	student book pages 18–19
6 **Understanding main points and ideas**	Identify the main points and ideas and how they are presented in a variety of texts.	Find and understand a text's main ideas.	Students identify the main idea of the whole text by looking at the features. They then look in detail at each paragraph to distinguish the main points contained within the text.	student book pages 20–21
7 **Identifying details**	Read and understand texts in detail.	Identify details in a text.	Students look for features, scan for key words and read closely to identify details within a text. They then use their skills to answer a series of questions based on a text.	student book pages 22–23

© Pearson Education Limited 2010 1

Schemes of work

Lesson	Aim	Learning objective	Activities	Resources
8 Understanding texts in detail	Read and understand texts in detail. Utilise information contained in texts.	Understand the main points and the details in a text.	Students explore texts in detail, reading sentences and paragraphs closely and using pictures, headings and captions to help them understand the meaning of the text.	student book pages 24–25
9 Identifying how texts are presented	Identify how the main points and ideas are presented in a variety of texts.	Identify the different presentation features used in a text. Understand why they are used.	Students look at a range of texts to identify presentational features, exploring how they help the writer to convey their ideas to the reader.	student book page 26–27
10 Understanding how texts are presented	Read and understand texts in detail. Identify the main points and ideas and how they are presented in a variety of texts.	Understand presentation features. Explain what effect they have on readers.	Students look at presentational features in more detail, understanding how they enhance the text and the effect they have on the reader. Students then answer questions about the presentational features of the text.	student book pages 28–29
11 Finding information in tables	Read, understand and utilise information contained in tables.	Find and use information presented in tables.	Students are presented with various table formats, which they learn to read accurately to answer questions based on information within the tables.	student book pages 30–31
12 Finding information in charts	Read, understand and utilise information contained in charts.	Find and use information presented in charts.	Students are presented with pie charts and bar charts, which they learn to read accurately to answer questions based on information within the charts.	student book pages 32–33
13 Reading a text and responding to it	Read and understand texts in detail. Identify suitable responses to texts.	Decide how to respond to a text.	Students learn to decide how to respond to a text, looking for instructions and planning a suitable response.	student book pages 34–35

2 © Pearson Education Limited 2010

Schemes of work

Speaking, listening and communication

Introduction to the scheme of work for Speaking, listening and communication

Functional English Level 1 Speaking, listening and communication helps students to develop their skills in contributing to formal and informal discussions.

Level 1 skill standard for Speaking, listening and communication: take full part in formal and informal discussions and exchanges that include unfamiliar subjects. These skills help students to:

- make relevant and extended contributions to discussions, allowing for and responding to others' input
- prepare for and contribute to the formal discussion of ideas and opinions
- make different kinds of contributions to discussions
- present information/points of view clearly and in appropriate language.

Lesson	Aim	Learning objective	Activities	Resources
1 Taking part in an informal discussion	Make relevant and extended contributions to informal discussion, allowing for and responding to others' input. Present information/points of view clearly and in appropriate language.	Prepare for a discussion. Make clear, relevant contributions. Listen to others.	Students prepare for an informal discussion. They learn to plan their points, make relevant contributions and actively listen to others. They then hold the informal discussion and assess how they can improve their skills.	student book pages 46–49
2 Taking part in a formal discussion	Prepare for and contribute to the formal discussion of ideas and opinions. Make different kinds of contributions to discussions. Present information/points of view clearly and in appropriate language.	Prepare for a discussion. Take part in a formal discussion, adopting different roles.	Students prepare for a formal discussion. They learn about different roles, e.g. chair, and write an agenda to structure their discussion. They then hold their formal discussion and assess how they can improve their skills.	student book pages 50–53

© Pearson Education Limited 2010   3

Schemes of work

Writing

Introduction to the scheme of work for Writing

Functional English Level 1 Writing develops students' writing skills in range of texts and contexts.

Level 1 skill standard for Writing: write a range of texts to communicate information, ideas and opinions, using formats and styles suitable for their purpose and audience. These skills help students to:

- write clearly and coherently, including an appropriate level of detail
- present information in a logical sequence
- use language, format and structure suitable for purpose and audience
- use correct grammar, including correct and consistent use of tense
- ensure written work includes generally accurate punctuation and spelling and that meaning is clear.

Lesson	Aim	Learning objective	Activities	Resources
1 Writing for your audience	Use language, format and structure suitable for the audience.	Suit your writing to your audience.	Students learn how to suit their writing to their audience. Students are then presented with scenarios, from which they identify the prospective audience and then ensure their writing is fit for purpose.	student book pages 62–63
2 Writing to suit a purpose	Use language, format and structure suitable for the purpose.	Suit your writing to your purpose.	Students learn what to include in their writing to achieve their purpose, incorporating facts and opinions.	student book pages 64–67
3 Understanding form	Write clearly and coherently using appropriate form.	Choose the right form for your writing and use the right features.	Students look at different forms of writing and learn about what features the different forms of writing contain. They then learn how to use these features correctly and effectively in their own writing.	student book page 68–73
4 Understanding style	Ensure written work includes generally accurate punctuation and spelling and that meaning is clear.	Suit your writing style to your purpose and audience.	Students learn how to suit their writing to their audience using a particular style, e.g. formal or informal. Students redraft texts to improve style and learn how to use apostrophes correctly.	student book pages 74–77
5 Planning and organising your writing	Present information in a logical sequence.	Read writing tasks carefully to work out what you must do. Plan your texts appropriately.	Students learn how to plan and organise their writing, paying particular attention to audience, purpose, form and style. They practise making plans and use them to write responses to tasks.	student book pages 78–81

Schemes of work

6 Writing in paragraphs	Write clearly and coherently, including an appropriate level of detail. Use correct grammar, including correct and consistent use of tense.	Plan and write well-structured paragraphs. Link your paragraphs together.	Students read a sample text and identify the main paragraphs and learn how to structure paragraphs using the 'PEEL' method. They then learn how to link their paragraphs together using connectives.	student book pages 82–85
7 Using main points and details	Ensure written work includes generally accurate punctuation and spelling and that meaning is clear.	Work out the difference between a main point and detail. Use both main points and details in your paragraphs. Practise planning and writing paragraphs.	Students learn how to distinguish between main points and details in texts. They then plan and write paragraphs to include details, main points and connectives in their writing. Students also learn how to use inverted commas correctly.	student book pages 86–89
8 Writing effective sentences	Use correct grammar, including correct and consistent use of tense.	Write in complete and clear sentences. Write in different types of sentences and punctuate sentences correctly.	Students learn about writing simple sentences to include a verb and correct punctuation. They learn how to vary their sentences to make them more interesting and how to use punctuation to help readers understand the meaning of their text.	student book pages 90–93
9 Practising writing clearly and logically (1)	Write clearly and coherently, including an appropriate level of detail. Present information in a logical sequence.	Practise writing a complete text. Organise points logically and improve spelling.	Students learn how to write instructions clearly using time connectives to link their points together. They also focus on how to improve their spelling in order for their writing to be accurate and effective.	student book pages 94–97
10 Practising writing clearly and logically (2)	Use language, format and structure suitable for purpose and audience. Use correct grammar, including correct and consistent use of tense. Ensure written work includes generally accurate punctuation and spelling and that meaning is clear.	Practise writing a complete text in the form of briefing notes. Organise points logically and use correct verb tenses.	Students learn how to write briefing notes by planning and organising their points, incorporating headings and separating sections with bullet points. They prepare draft briefing notes in response to a task, learn how to use correct verb tenses and rewrite their draft to check they have included the correct tenses in their writing.	student book pages 98–101

Key Stage 3 matching grids

Introduction

Functional Skills English is taught through the English programmes of study. There are important distinctions that need to be observed, however, such as the key concept of competence as this has clear links with functionality. Competence is defined as *being clear and coherent in spoken and written communication*. The areas of the programmes of study that reflect Functional English have been identified and mapped to the skill standard and aim to assist you in planning your teaching programme.

Reading

The need to understand texts in their different forms has been recognised as essential to equip students with life skills. Essentially, reading and its assessment in Functional English focus on texts that are grounded in real-life contexts; responses to these will reflect situations in life, rather than an empathetic response. The texts in Functional Reading must have realistic contexts, and responses must demonstrate the skills as identified in the aims. The acquisition of these skills is responding to society's need for its members to make informed judgements and frame appropriate responses within realistic contexts. You will notice that texts used for assessment of Functional Skills in reading are authentic, drawn from a range of documents such as leaflets, articles, guidance documents, letters and web pages. The KS3 programme of study also refers to texts taken from real-life contexts and functional purposes.

The mapped areas from the programme of study refer to texts and to reading in a real-life context. The study of, and responses to, literary texts are assessed in GCSE English and GCSE English Literature. At Level 1, students must demonstrate the ability to identify the main points and their presentation in a variety of texts. They must also go beyond simply reading a text and show that they understand it in detail, demonstrating that they can apply their reading skills by utilising the information in texts and identifying suitable responses. Students need to read and understand texts written in different forms and for different purposes, while continuing to study literary texts drawn from different genres, cultures and times. The mapping includes references from the programmes of study to both form and purpose, as well as the corresponding exemplification to illustrate the importance of functionality in the National Curriculum and its direct correlation with reading in Functional English.

Speaking, listening and communication

At Level 1, students must show that they are competent in informal and formal discussions and exchanges that include unfamiliar subjects. They need to make relevant and extended contributions to discussions. They are also assessed on their success in enabling others to contribute and on making appropriate responses to those contributions. Students should also demonstrate that they can communicate clearly and use appropriate language. Competence in the programmes of study also means *being adaptable in a widening range of familiar and unfamiliar contexts*, and this extends beyond the learning environment. The application of Speaking, listening and communication skills to real-life situations is a requirement in the programmes of study as well as in Functional English, and is identified in the mapping; this makes co-teaching these aspects of the programmes of study with the aims in the Functional Skills criteria both viable and logical. Additionally, communicating either formally and informally will be decided through *informed choices*, again a feature of both. Using speaking and listening for dramatic effect or for literary presentations has its place in the KS3 English programmes of study, but not in preparing students to be *functional*, so this would be taught separately and seen by the students as distinct from their work in Functional English.

Writing

Writing contexts must be grounded in reality and should reflect the types of writing that will be necessary in the world of work and society in general. Section 2.3 of the KS3 programmes of study makes *composition* its focus; this refers to many features that are recognisably functional. The references to aspects linked with creative responses have been removed for the purposes of this guidance. While these continue to be an essential part of the English curriculum, they are not part of the skills standard and the aims in the *Functional Skills criteria for English* document.

As with the aims, the composition section of the programme of study places emphasis on clarity, adapting writing for audience and purpose, using a range of sentence structures and ensuring that writing suits its purpose. Significant importance is given to technical accuracy in the programmes of study, and 40–45% of the assessment in the standards concerns accuracy. As with the other two components, writing tasks must be contextualised and rooted in authentic real-life situations. It is essential that students answer each task as closely as possible. If asked to write a formal letter, for example, they must present their response using the appropriate layout and tone/register. In Section 4.3 of the programme of study the explanatory notes expand on writing for contexts and purposes beyond the classroom, providing guidance in applying writing skills to real life. To be competent in Level 1 Writing, students must demonstrate this ability more than once, usually employing a different form, audience and purpose each time. They also need to write clearly using an appropriate level of detail, sequence their work logically and demonstrate control of spelling, punctuation and grammar. In the programme of study the identified forms of writing that would be potentially functional include articles, letters, reports and commentaries.

The student has to pass each component in order to be awarded a Functional English level. The mapping is designed to illustrate how specified aspects of the programmes of study can be mapped to the aims in Functional English. It is essential to deliver a teaching programme that targets Functional Skills in English as part of the curriculum. An important message to emerge from this qualification in its pilot stage is that the more successful learners are those who have been carefully prepared for what is a highly specified qualification.

Functional Skills mapping

Reading

The tables below show how the Functional Skills are linked to the Key Stage 3 programmes of study.

<table>
<tr><td rowspan="6">Functional Skills</td><td>SB pages</td><td>6–43</td></tr>
<tr><td>Level</td><td>1</td></tr>
<tr><td>Skill standard</td><td>Read and understand a range of straightforward texts.</td></tr>
<tr><td rowspan="5">Aim</td><td>Identify the main points and ideas and how they are presented in a variety of texts.</td></tr>
<tr><td>Read and understand texts in detail.</td></tr>
<tr><td>Utilise information contained in the texts.</td></tr>
<tr><td>Identify suitable responses to texts.</td></tr>
<tr><td>In more than one type of text.</td></tr>
<tr><td rowspan="3">Links to KS3 Programme of Study</td><td colspan="2">Engage with ideas and texts, understanding and responding to the main issues.
Extract and interpret information, events, main points and ideas from texts.
Understand how audiences and readers choose and respond to texts.
Understand how the nature and purpose of texts influences the selection of content and its meanings.
How form, layout and presentation contribute to effect.
Forms such as journalism, travel writing, essays, reportage, literary non-fiction and multimodal texts including film.
Purposes such as to instruct, inform, explain, describe, analyse, review, discuss and persuade.</td></tr>
<tr><td colspan="2">**Level 4**
In responding to a range of texts, students show understanding of significant ideas, themes, events and characters, beginning to use inference and deduction. They understand that texts reflect the time and culture in which they were written. They refer to the text when explaining their views and are able to locate and use ideas and information.</td></tr>
<tr><td colspan="2">**Level 5**
Students show understanding of a range of texts, selecting essential points and using inference and deduction where appropriate. In their responses, they identify key features, themes and characters and select sentences, phrases and relevant information to support their views. They understand that texts fit into historical and literary traditions. They retrieve and collate information from a range of sources.</td></tr>
</table>

Speaking, listening and communication

Functional Skills mapping

Functional Skills	SB pages	44–57
	Level	1
	Skill standard	Take full part in formal and informal discussions/exchanges.
	Aim	Make relevant and extended contributions to discussions, allowing for and responding to others' input.
		Prepare for and contribute to the formal discussion of ideas and opinions.
		Make different kinds of contributions to discussions.
		Present information/points of view clearly and in appropriate language.

Links to KS3 Programme of Study

Present information and points of view clearly and appropriately in different contexts.

Adapt talk for a range of purposes and audiences, including the more formal.

Listen and respond constructively to others, taking different views into account and modifying their own views in the light of what others say.

Make different kinds of relevant contributions in groups, responding appropriately to others, proposing ideas and asking questions.

Level 4

Students talk and listen with confidence in an increasing range of contexts. Their talk is adapted to the purpose: developing ideas thoughtfully, describing events and conveying their opinions clearly. They listen carefully in discussions, making contributions and asking questions that are responsive to others' ideas and views. They adapt their spoken language appropriately and use some of the features of standard English vocabulary and grammar.

Level 5

Students talk and listen confidently in a wide range of contexts, including some that are formal. Their talk engages the interest of the listener as they begin to vary their expression and vocabulary. In discussions, they pay close attention to what others say, ask questions to develop ideas and make contributions that take account of others' views. They adapt their spoken language to suit the situation and begin to use standard English in formal situations.

Functional Skills mapping

Writing

<table>
<tr><td rowspan="3">Functional Skills</td><td>SB pages</td><td>58–109</td></tr>
<tr><td>Level</td><td>1</td></tr>
<tr><td>Skill standard</td><td>Write a range of texts to communicate information, ideas and opinions, using formats and styles suitable for their purpose and audience.</td></tr>
<tr><td></td><td>Aim</td><td>Write clearly and coherently, including an appropriate level of detail.
Present information in a logical sequence.
Use language, format and structure suitable for purpose and audience.
Use correct grammar, including correct and consistent use of tense.
Ensure written work includes generally accurate punctuation and spelling and that meaning is clear.</td></tr>
</table>

Links to KS3 Programme of Study	
	Write clearly and coherently, including an appropriate level of detail.
	Adapt style and language appropriately for a range of forms, purposes and readers.
	Structure their writing to support the purpose of the task and guide the reader.
	Use clearly demarcated paragraphs to organise meaning.
	Use complex sentences to extend, link and develop ideas.
	Vary sentence structure for interest, effect and subtleties of meaning.
	Consider what the reader needs to know and include relevant details.
	Present material clearly, using appropriate layout, and organisation.
	Write for contexts and purposes beyond the classroom.

Level 4

Students' writing in a range of forms is lively and thoughtful. Ideas are often sustained and developed in interesting ways, with organisation generally appropriate for purpose. Vocabulary choices are often adventurous and words are used for effect. Students are beginning to use grammatically complex sentences, extending meaning. Spelling, including that of polysyllabic words that conform to regular patterns, is generally accurate. Full stops, capital letters and question marks are used correctly, and students are beginning to use punctuation within sentences. Handwriting style is fluent, joined and legible.

Level 5

Students' writing is varied and interesting, conveying meaning clearly in a range of forms for different readers, using a more formal style where appropriate. Vocabulary choices are imaginative and words are used precisely. Sentences, including complex ones, and paragraphs are coherent, clear and well developed. Words with complex regular patterns are usually spelt correctly. A range of punctuation, including commas, apostrophes and inverted commas, is usually used accurately. Handwriting is joined, clear and fluent and, where appropriate, is adapted to a range of tasks.

GCSE matching grids

Introduction

The National Curriculum English programmes of study include Functional English. 'In studying English, students develop skills in speaking, listening, communicating, reading and writing that they will need to participate in society and employment.' This statement, taken from 'The importance of English' in the programme of study for Key Stage 4, makes a clear link with functionality and one of the key concepts identified and exemplified is competence. The five areas identified are entirely functional in their focus. Functional English can be co-taught with GCSE English and English Language, and this is demonstrated in the mapping of the three Functional English components to the Edexcel English/English Language GCSE Unit 3.

Reading

In GCSE English and English Language, students are required to respond to a range of literary and non-literary texts. The key difference between GCSE and Functional English is that the latter does not cover literary texts. The similarities in the assessment requirements demonstrate that there is a significant overlap in terms of responding to non-literary texts, and this is what makes co-teaching viable and enables an integrated approach to teaching.

Level 1 requires students to identify main points and ideas and how they are presented in a variety of texts, and to read and understand texts in detail. Students also need to demonstrate that they can apply their reading skills in realistic contexts by utilising the information in texts and identifying suitable responses. The GCSE criteria, drawn from the programme of study, require that students demonstrate the ability to read and understand texts, select material appropriate to purpose, collate from different sources, making comparisons and cross-references as appropriate. They should also be able to explain and evaluate how writers use linguistic and grammatical features to achieve effects and engage and influence the reader. The mapping shows that this is also assessed in Functional Reading.

There is continuing recognition of the need for students to read and understand texts written in different forms and for different purposes, while continuing to study literary texts drawn from different genres, cultures and times. Essentially, texts in Functional Reading assessments are grounded in real-life contexts and responses need to be appropriately framed within these. The texts used for assessment of Functional Skills are drawn from the range of documents we encounter in real life, such as leaflets, articles, guidance documents, letters and web pages. These also feature in GCSE and require students to make appropriate responses. The programme of study identifies the need for students to understand the origin and purpose of texts from a range of sources, including websites.

Speaking, listening and communication

In Functional English, students need to be competent in both familiar and unfamiliar contexts. In Level 1 there are two areas for assessment: informal and formal discussion. Students are required to make relevant and extended contributions and respect and respond to the contributions of others. They need to prepare for and contribute to discussions, make different kinds of contributions and use appropriate language. These skills are identified in Section 2.1 of the programme of study, where students need to demonstrate the ability to listen to complex information, make cogent responses, present information clearly, use a range of strategies and sustain discussion in different contexts. The GCSE subject criteria require candidates to communicate purposefully, structure and sustain talk, adapting it to different situations and audiences, use standard English and a variety of techniques as appropriate, and listen and respond to speakers' ideas and perspectives.

The main difference between GCSE and Functional Skills is in creating and sustaining roles. In GCSE, this includes creating a dramatic role involving the imagination. In Functional English, it refers to roles that are grounded in real-life contexts, such as chairing a discussion or interviewing someone. It is possible to co-teach to prepare students for assessments in both qualifications and assess any dramatic elements for GCSE separately. The overlap with GCSE English is in discussion and communication. It would be logical to assess participation in different types of discussion for co-teaching Functional English and GCSE and separately assess any imaginative role play, such as undertaking a role drawn from a literary text.

© Pearson Education Limited 2010

Functional Skills mapping

Writing

Similarly, in the area of writing, contexts must be grounded in reality and students' writing should reflect the types of writing that will be necessary in the world of work and society in general. The features of writing for Functional English need to be recognisably functional. Audience, form and purpose need to reflect the types of writing we need to produce in the real world. The GCSE criteria require candidates to write to communicate clearly, effectively and imaginatively, using and adapting forms and selecting vocabulary appropriately to task and purpose in ways that engage the reader. Where GCSE and Functional English differ is in any form of imaginative writing. This has a valuable place in English teaching, but needs to be taught as distinct from the requirements for writing functional documents. In both GCSE and Functional Writing, candidates must organise information and ideas into structured and sequenced sentences, paragraphs and texts. They need to use a variety of linguistic and structural features to support cohesion and overall coherence. They will need to demonstrate the ability to use a range of sentence structures for clarity, purpose and effect, with accurate punctuation and spelling. Correspondingly, at Level 1, students must use correct grammar, including tenses, and ensure that punctuation and spelling are generally accurate and that the meaning is clear. The references to aspects of writing linked with creative responses have been removed for the purposes of this guidance. While these continue to be an essential part of the English curriculum, they are not part of the skills standard and the aims in the Functional Skills criteria for English document.

As with the aims, the composition section of the programme of study places emphasis on fluent writing, presenting information on complex subjects, using a range of ways to structure whole texts and a variety of persuasive techniques and sentence structures. Importance is given to technical accuracy in the programme of study; this is also evident in the standards, where 40–45% of the assessment concerns accuracy. Like the other two components, writing tasks must be contextualised and rooted in authentic real-life situations. To be competent in Level 1 writing, students must demonstrate the ability to write clearly and coherently with appropriate detail. They must present information in a logical sequence and use language, format and structure suitable for purpose and audience. In the programme of study, forms of writing that would be potentially functional include articles, letters, reports and commentaries (see section 3.3 for the full range identified).

The student has to pass each component in order to be awarded a Functional English qualification at Level 1. The mapping is designed to illustrate how specified aspects of the programme of study can be mapped to the aims in Functional English. It is essential to deliver a teaching programme that targets Functional Skills in English as part of the curriculum.

GCSE and Level 1 mapping

Functional Skills mapping

Reading

Functional Skills

SB pages	Level	Skill standard	Aim	Assessment objective	Content	Links to Edexcel English/English Language GCSE Unit 1 — Grade description
6–43	1	Read and understand a range of straightforward texts.	Identify the main points and ideas and how they are presented in a variety of texts. Read and understand texts in detail. Utilise information contained in texts. Identify suitable responses to texts. **In more than one type of text.**	(i) Read and understand texts, selecting material appropriate to purpose, collating from different sources and making comparisons and cross-references as appropriate. (ii) Develop and sustain interpretations of writers' ideas and perspectives, referring closely to the development of narrative, argument, explanation or analysis. (iii) Explain and evaluate how writers use linguistic, grammatical, structural and presentational features to achieve effects and engage and influence the reader, supporting their comments with detailed textual references.	Understand how meaning is constructed through words, sentences and whole texts, recognising and responding to the effects of language variation. Evaluate the ways in which texts may be interpreted differently according to the perspective of the reader.	**F** Candidates describe the main ideas, themes or arguments in a range of texts and refer to specific aspects or details when justifying their views. They make simple comparisons and cross-references that show some awareness of how texts achieve their effects through writers' use of linguistic, grammatical, structural and presentational devices. **C** Candidates understand and demonstrate how meaning and information are conveyed in a range of texts. They make personal and critical responses, referring to specific aspects of language, grammar, structure and presentational devices to justify their views. They successfully compare and cross-reference aspects of texts and explain convincingly how they may vary in purpose and how they achieve different effects.

© Pearson Education Limited 2010   13

Functional Skills mapping

Speaking, listening and communication

Functional Skills					Links to Edexcel English/ English Language GCSE Unit 1
SB pages	Level	Skill standard	Aim	Assessment objective	Content	Grade description
44–57	1	Take full part in formal and informal discussions and exchanges that include unfamiliar subjects.	Make relevant and extended contributions to discussions, allowing for and responding to others' input. Prepare for and contribute to the formal discussion of ideas and opinions. Make different kinds of contributions to discussions. Present information/ points of view clearly and in appropriate language. **In formal and informal exchanges and discussions.**	(i) Communicate clearly and purposefully; structure and sustain talk, adapting it to different situations and audiences; use standard English and a variety of techniques as appropriate. (ii) Listen and respond to speakers' ideas, perspectives and how they construct and express their meanings. (iii) Interact with others, shaping meanings through suggestions, comments and questions and drawing ideas together. (iv) Create and sustain different roles.	Present and listen to information and ideas. Respond to the questions and views of others, adapting talk appropriately to context and audience. Make a range of effective contributions, using creative approaches to exploring questions, solving problems and developing ideas. Reflect and comment critically on their own and others' uses of language. Participate in a range of contexts, including real-life uses of talk and audiences beyond the classroom.	**F** Candidates talk confidently in familiar situations, showing some awareness of purpose and of listeners' needs. They convey information, develop ideas and describe feelings clearly, using the main features of standard English as appropriate. They listen with concentration and make relevant responses to others' ideas and opinions. In formal and creative activities, they attempt to meet the demands of different roles. **C** Candidates adapt their talk to the demands of different situations and contexts. They recognise when standard English is required and use it confidently. They use different sentence structures and select vocabulary so that information, ideas and feelings are communicated clearly and the listener's interest is engaged. Through careful listening and by developing their own and others' ideas, they make significant contributions to discussion and participate effectively in creative activities.

14 © Pearson Education Limited 2010

Writing

Functional Skills

SB pages	Level	Skill standard	Aim	Assessment objective	Content	Links to Edexcel English/English Language GCSE Unit 1 Grade description
58–109	1	Write a range of texts to communicate information, ideas and opinions, using formats and styles suitable for their purpose and audience.	Write clearly and coherently, including an appropriate level of detail. Present information in a logical sequence. Use language format and structure suitable for purpose and audience. (55–60%) Use correct grammar, including correct and consistent use of tense. Ensure written work includes generally accurate punctuation and spelling and that meaning is clear. (40–45%) **In more than one type of text.**	(i) Communicate clearly, effectively and imaginatively, using and adapting forms and selecting vocabulary appropriate to task and purpose in ways which engage the reader. (ii) Organise information and ideas into well-structured and sequenced sentences, paragraphs and whole texts, using a variety of linguistic and structural features to support cohesion and overall competence. (iii) Use a range of sentence structures for clarity, purpose and effect with accurate punctuation and spelling.	Write accurately and fluently, choosing content and adapting style and language to a wide range of forms, media and contexts, audience and purposes.	**F** Candidates' writing shows some adaptation of form and style for different tasks and purposes. It communicates simply and clearly with the reader. Sentences sequence events or ideas logically; vocabulary is sometimes chosen for variety and interest. Paragraphing is straightforward but effective; the structure of sentences, including some that are complex, is usually correct. Spelling and basic punctuation are mostly accurate. **C** Candidates' writing shows successful adaptation of form and style to different tasks and for various purposes. They use a range of sentences structures and varied vocabulary to create different effects and engage the reader's interest. Paragraphing is used effectively to make the sequence of events or development of ideas coherent and clear to the reader. Sentence structures are varied; punctuation and spelling are accurate and sometimes bold.

© Pearson Education Limited 2010

Functional Skills mapping

Skills checklist

This self-assessment tool is designed so that your students can use it to help them identify areas of strength and areas that need development. It is adapted from the criteria, but broken down into smaller sections so that students can rate specific aspects of their performances in each of the three components. This will help them to be discerning in their identification of areas needing improvement. You may want to introduce each of the components alongside the introductory notes in the student book for Reading, Speaking, listening and communication and Writing so that your students are negotiating one aspect of the qualification and their self-assessment at a time. As part of your introduction to the skills checklists, you might encourage them to discuss each aspect (with peers and then as a class) so that they fully understand them. The rating out of 10 and the 'comments' section may also be useful as part of any formative assessment system and individual target setting.

Reading

I can:	I need more work on this 1–4	I am OK but need a little more work 5–7	I am confident that I can do this 8–10	/10	Comments
Identify main points and ideas in texts					
Identify how points and ideas are presented in texts					
Read texts in detail					
Show I understand texts in detail					
Utilise (make use of) information in texts					
Identify suitable responses to texts					

© Pearson Education Limited 2010

Speaking, listening and communication

I can:	I need more work on this 1–4	I am OK but need a little more work 5–7	I am confident that I can do this 8–10	/10	Comments
Make contributions that keep to the point					
Make contributions that I can develop					
Respond to the comments made by others					
Prepare for formal discussion of ideas/opinions					
Contribute to formal discussions of ideas/opinions					
Make different kinds of contributions to discussions					
Present information and points of view clearly					
Use appropriate language in discussions					

© Pearson Education Limited 2010

Writing

I can:	I need more work on this 1–4	I am OK but need a little more work 5–7	I am confident that I can do this 8–10	/10	Comments
Write clearly so that what I write makes sense					
Present information in a logical sequence					
Use language suitable for purpose and audience					
Use form (format) suitable for purpose and audience					
Use structure suitable for purpose and audience					
Use correct grammar					
Use correct tenses consistently					
Punctuate mostly correctly					
Spell mostly accurately					
Write so that what I mean is clear					

Functional Skills English Level 1 student book at a glance

Functional Skills mapping

READING

Skill standard	Aim	Student book pages
1 Reading a range of texts	Learn to read different types of texts.	8–11
2 Working out what a text is about	Read and understand the points and ideas in a text.	12–13
3 Finding the information you need in a text	Use different techniques to search for information in texts.	14–15
4 Reading closely for detailed understanding	Read a text closely to understand texts in detail.	16–17
5 Identifying the main point in a paragraph	Identify the main points and how they are presented in a variety of texts.	18–19
6 Understanding main points and ideas	Identify the main points and ideas and how they are presented in a variety of texts.	20–21
7 Identifying details	Read and understand texts in detail.	22–23
8 Understanding texts in detail	Read and understand texts in detail. Utilise information contained in texts.	24–25
9 Identifying how texts are presented	Identify how the main points and ideas are presented in a variety of texts.	26–27
10 Understanding how texts are presented	Read and understand texts in detail. Identify the main points and ideas and how they are presented in a variety of texts.	28–29
11 Finding information in tables	Read, understand and utilise information contained in tables.	30–31
12 Finding information in charts	Read, understand and utilise information contained in charts.	32–33
13 Reading a text and responding to it	Read and understand texts in detail. Identify suitable responses to texts.	34–35

SPEAKING, LISTENING AND COMMUNICATION

Skill standard	Aim	Student book pages
1 Taking part in an informal discussion	Make relevant and extended contributions to informal discussion, allowing for and responding to others' input. Present information/points of view clearly and in appropriate language.	46–49
2 Taking part in a formal discussion	Prepare for and contribute to the formal discussion of ideas and opinions. Make different kinds of contributions to discussions. Present information/points of view clearly and in appropriate language.	50–53

© Pearson Education Limited 2010   19

WRITING

Skill standard	Aim	Student book pages
1 Writing for your audience	Use language, format and structure suitable for the audience.	62–63
2 Writing to suit a purpose	Use language, format and structure suitable for the purpose.	64–67
3 Understanding form	Write clearly and coherently using appropriate form.	68–73
4 Understanding style	Ensure written work includes generally accurate punctuation and spelling and that meaning is clear.	74–77
5 Planning and organising your writing	Present information in a logical sequence.	78–81
6 Writing in paragraphs	Write clearly and coherently, including an appropriate level of detail. Use correct grammar, including correct and consistent use of tense.	82–85
7 Using main points and details	Ensure written work includes generally accurate punctuation and spelling and that meaning is clear.	86–89
8 Writing effective sentences	Use correct grammar, including correct and consistent use of tense.	90–93
9 Practising writing clearly and logically (1)	Write clearly and coherently, including an appropriate level of detail. Present information in a logical sequence.	94–97
10 Practising writing clearly and logically (2)	Use language, format and structure suitable for purpose and audience. Use correct grammar, including correct and consistent use of tense. Ensure written work includes generally accurate punctuation and spelling and that meaning is clear.	98–101

Approaches to teaching Reading

Introduction

The Reading section of the Level 1 student book targets all of the skills standards and aims required for the teaching of Level 1 Reading. It provides a range of source materials and activities to prepare students for the Reading paper. The introductory pages are there to help your students, and they will benefit from you taking them through the introduction, the self-assessment information and the way in which they will be assessed in the examination.

Also in this section the 'standards' are printed for their reference (see page 7 of the student book) and there will be opportunities to reinforce what is expected of them during the reading lessons that follow.

Reading is divided into thirteen sections, each with the learning objectives clearly stated in the 'this lesson will help you to' box at the start. There is further explanation where necessary, as well as guidance which will often act as a useful checklist to help students reinforce their learning and for revision purposes.

It is important to explain to students that Reading is one of three components that they need to pass in order to gain a Level 1 qualification in Functional English. Use the opportunities as they present themselves in the lessons to refer to the structure of the question paper, including texts, question types and rubric.

The lessons

The lesson plans contained in this teacher guide are directly based on the sections in the student book: resources are provided to support teaching and learning, and the activities will help students to become confident readers at Level 1 and act as preparation for their assessment. In some lesson plans, it is suggested that additional resources are used to support some of the activities.

Encourage students to make connections between lessons, as this will help them to contextualise their learning and develop transferable skills.

Helping students to engage with the texts

In order to become confident readers, students need to engage in reading as an active process. On many occasions in the lesson plans, it is suggested that copies of the text are made so that students can annotate, highlight and underline as they carry out the activities in the student book. This is helpful to the reading process and can be used to reinforce learning in feedback to their peers. Encourage students to make brief notes as they read, focusing on:

- words/phrases that help them to answer a question
- words that need their meaning clarified
- topic sentences in paragraphs
- identifying main points/ideas that link with the purpose of paragraphs
- connectives that link ideas and will help them to see how ideas are linked in a text
- features of a text.

Modelling reading skills/how to be an active reader

Particularly in the early lessons, modelling how to read and understand different text types and purposes is a useful teaching tool. For example, in Lesson 1, model reading of Text A to your students, talking through your thought processes as you do so. This will be useful for a number of reasons: you can talk them through the form required for a formal letter; this will help them to understand how the text is presented and will help them when they have to write a formal letter as part of the Writing component. Also, as the form is in silhouette, modelling it with them will help to clarify the form itself and how to approach a text to establish its form. There are opportunities for students to work in groups and independently, and to share their ideas in whole-class discussions. Where it is recommended that you take students through a task or a text, sharing your own thought processes with them will help them to become increasingly independent readers.

You could use an overhead or digital projector for modelling your reading skills and explain:

- how you read a task/question
- what reading skills you are using and why
- how you make sense of difficult/unfamiliar words
- how to solve problems with a question by engaging with the text in order to overcome any obstacles.

Identify the main points and ideas

A good starting point is to ask students to identify the main purpose of a text. This is a feature of our Reading assessments as exemplified in the sample assessment materials. It is also part of the skills standard, as students need to be able to identify the main points.

Reading lesson plans

Identify the main points and ideas and how they are presented in a variety of texts

Lesson 1 includes a range of useful text types for students to establish how main points and ideas are presented. Throughout the Reading lessons there are questions that ask students to demonstrate this skill. A combination of independent, collaborative and teacher-mediated activities will help them to be proficient. As students progress, they will explore features that make a text a particular text type. This is reinforced in the Writing lessons, where texts are provided as the basis for students to develop their own writing skills. Use opportunities as they present themselves to engage students with the main points/ideas and presentational features of texts. Encourage them to ask themselves questions about the effect of layout, use of language, uses of bullets, paragraphing and images. Encourage them also to consider different ways of presenting information, such as tables. Take them through the uses of keys, symbols, titles and headings.

Read and understand texts in detail

There are many opportunities for students to engage in close reading through the activities in the student book and the corresponding lesson plans. Where you model your own reading, you will also be drawing their attention to the appropriate detail. Where possible, provide separate copies of texts as suggested in the lesson plans so that students can annotate and work with the text, focusing on details as required. Annotated texts can later be displayed for revision purposes. Ask students to bring to the lesson examples of other texts that they have worked on, as a preparation for further reading for detail. Encourage students to annotate their texts collaboratively and to share their ideas with the rest of the class through discussion and display.

Utilise information contained in texts

Lessons 4–12 of the student book contain opportunities for students to practise and develop their skills to utilise information. In your teaching, encourage them to regard reading as a dynamic activity, as in everyday life they read texts to make use of information. Invite students to think of and find examples of texts from which we select and utilise information. These can be shared in lessons, and discussions about how we utilise information will help to reinforce learning. Timetables, menus and television/cinema schedules are some sources that can be used for this purpose.

Identify suitable responses to texts

Supporting activities for this skill are provided in the final reading lesson. The ability to identify suitable responses requires more demanding application of reading skills, so it is advisable to teach this aspect of the 'standards' at a later stage in the course. Wherever possible, gather examples of texts that require some sort of action on the part of the reader, and ask students to find examples of their own. As a learning activity, students could show the others an example of such a text and explain the response that needs to made, e.g. donating clothes to charity, or collecting an undelivered package as shown in the student book.

Use of resources

As the course progresses, encourage students to bring in different text types to exemplify form, audience and purpose. These could be displayed as annotated collages to reinforce their learning. Again, where possible, use an OHP/digital projector to demonstrate key teaching points and encourage students to present their work to the class where appropriate, such as in the completion of activities in lesson 4. It is recommended in many of the lessons to make copies of some of the texts available in A4 or A3 so that students are able to highlight/underline/annotate to develop as active readers.

Preparing for the Reading component/test

The lessons in the student book contain resources to prepare students for the assessment. Encourage students to read the questions as closely as the source text, ensuring that they are familiar with the different styles of questioning. Teach them to look for key words in the question to help them to locate specific information/detail in the text. Draw their attention also to questions where the number of features required is specified, for example: 'Find **two** features that show that this text is from a web page.' Share mark schemes with the students as soon as possible. Use questions from the pilot, the sample assessment materials and the questions/activities provided in the student book. Use the sample reading assessment and mark scheme as definitive guidance for your students; they need to be familiar with the style of assessment, so you should share not only texts, questions and mark schemes with them, but also which part of the standard is being assessed.

Give students practice or 'mock' examination opportunities so that they become accustomed to responding appropriately and managing time.

Encourage students to make the links with their own Writing and with Speaking, listening and communication skills. They should also learn to make links with the Writing lessons as consideration of text types requires transferable skills. Although the three components are separately assessed, students need to understand that the language modes interrelate.

The lesson plans include opportunities for individual and collaborative learning. Working with their peers to a shared understanding is a powerful learning tool for students.

Reading lesson plans

1 Reading a range of texts

Aim
- Learn to read different types of texts.

Lesson learning and objectives
- Understand what kind of text you are reading. Find the information you need in a text.

Lesson starter: individual/pair work

Individually or in pairs, ask students to list as many different kinds of texts as they can on a sheet of A4 paper. Encourage them to regard texts in the broadest sense, e.g. the ingredients on a cereal packet. Take feedback in whole-class discussion and display the lists that students have produced.

Main teaching and learning

Direct students to page 8 of the student book and introduce the key concepts related to reading a range of texts and identifying different text types. Make sure they understand how to identify features and form in order to understand what information or ideas are given in the text.

Ask students to read **Activity 1** and take them through the outline of Text A. Model thinking aloud how to look at features, form, ideas and information. If possible, duplicate the Text B silhouette and ask pairs to identify the features, form, ideas and information. Through feedback, introduce the concepts of audience and purpose.

Move on to **Activity 2** on page 9 and make sure students understand the lists of features and forms. Direct pairs to look at Texts C to F (pages 9–11 of the student book) and link the particular features provided with each one. Pairs could present their findings to the class using A3/poster paper to identify each text, its purpose and audience, and the features that are representative of that particular text type.

Take whole-class feedback.

Plenary

Ask students to look at **Activity 3**. Discuss which texts Pia and Chang should read in order to find the information that they need. Extend the activity if necessary by asking students to make explicit links between text types and purpose. Point out the Top tip box on page 9 of the student book for useful advice.

Homework

Ask students to bring in at least one example of a text type to share with the class. You may want them to work in pairs and be prepared to present ideas to the class. Presentation should be in the form of question/answer and brief discussion, as this will also help them in their preparations for Speaking, listening and communication. (Presentations are not a requirement at Level 1.)

Answers

Activity 1
2 Text A is a letter; Text B is a magazine/newspaper article.

Activity 2
2 Slogan and image.
3 a Poster.
  b Text C is a poster because it has a large picture and a slogan but less text than a letter or product packaging.

Activity 3
2 Text D includes paragraphs and headings.
  Text E includes charts, lists and an image.
  Text F includes greetings and an image.
3 a Text D is a briefing note.
    Text E is product packaging.
    Text F is a letter.
  b Text D is a briefing note because it includes paragraphs but no images, and uses lists to convey information.
    Text E is product packaging because it includes an image to make it look nicer for consumers, and charts and lists to convey information about ingredients and the product.
    Text F is a letter because it uses a clear greeting and an appropriate sign-off.
4 a Text D.
  b The 'Nutritional info' chart.

2 Working out what a text is about

Aim
- Read and understand the points and ideas in a text.

Lesson learning and objectives
- Work out what a text is about and what its purpose is.

Lesson starter: individual/pair work

For the Starter activity, give students copies of a short text of your choice or choose a text from pages 12–13 of the student book. Make sure that the whole class engages with the same text.

Encourage students to engage in close reading and to read in pairs or threes, using the guidance in the introductory paragraph on page 12 of the student book – looking over every part of the text and asking what it is about and why it has been written.

For feedback, direct students to discuss 1) what the text is about, 2) its purpose and 3) the evidence for their decisions.

Main teaching and learning

Direct students to **Activity 1** and the Top tip box on page 12 and ask them to read Text A. In pairs, students discuss the multiple-choice options listed in question 2, and select what they consider to be the correct answer. Explain that selecting a text's main purpose from four choices is *one* style of question they will find on the Reading paper.

Use the opportunity to talk students through how they made their selection. You could ask them to discuss this in pairs or small groups.

Ask students to look at Text B and write an answer to **Activity 2**, question 2. Explain that they will be told in the examination that they do not have to write in sentences. Either explain the reason for this, or ask them to suggest a reason.

If possible, provide copies of Texts C and D on paper so that students can annotate them. Alternatively, provide paper and ask students to mind-map by putting Text C and later Text D in the centre and make notes on **Activity 3**, questions 2 and 3. Relate the questions to the relevant parts of the skills standard. Direct students to work in pairs. Take feedback, looking at Texts A to D and summarising form, audience and purpose.

Plenary

Share texts brought in as directed in the homework activity from the previous lesson.

Have a whole-class feedback session to discuss students' texts and their evidence for their ideas.

Homework

Ask students to find a text showing a food menu, such as a takeaway leaflet or restaurant menu, to bring to the next lesson.

Answers

Activity 1
2 C

Activity 2
2 The writer of Text B wants you to join a football team.

Activity 3
2 The writer of Text C wants you to sell your old DVDs, CDs, console games and/or videos to the company.
3 To persuade the consumer to purchase the products that they are retailing.

Reading lesson plans

3 Finding the information you need in a text

Aim
- Use different techniques to search for information in texts.

Lesson learning and objectives
- Use different ways of finding information in a text. Identify key words in a task. Find the key words in a text.

Lesson starter: individual/pair work

Before directing students to the student book, ask pairs to think of key words that link with the word 'pizza'. Make a class list of their suggestions.

Direct students to the 'This lesson will help you to' box on page 14 of the student book. Make sure that they recognise and distinguish between the elements listed. Draw their attention to the information and Top tip on page 14 concerning when they do or do not need to read every word of a text, but emphasise that close reading is also needed as a skill. Make links with the previous lessons.

Main teaching and learning

Encourage students to look closely at both the text and the questions in **Activity 1**. How well does the box of key words match their own ideas from the Starter activity? Go through the key words with them. Ask pairs or small groups to identify the words on a menu that indicate meat, cheese and hot spices. Ask them to group the words into the three categories, then take feedback.

Discuss with students how to deal with unfamiliar terms, e.g. process of elimination. Remind them that dictionaries are allowed and encourage their use.

Direct pairs or small groups to **Activity 2** and ask them to look at the words provided and work through questions 1, 2 and 3.

Direct students to look at Text A. You may wish to read the text together prior to students working through **Activity 3**. Encourage them to discuss their answers and the evidence they used before moving into the plenary.

Plenary

Ask students to share the food leaflets brought in as per the previous lesson's homework task. Discuss how the strategies used in the lesson could be used when reading 'real' texts. Have some spare leaflets available in case some students don't have one.

Go back to Text A. Encourage students to look at how the text is organised, including symbols and important additional information in brackets, e.g. regarding food allergies. Draw attention again to strategies used to gain information and discuss also how this is a useful reading skill in the 'real world'. Relate this to the food leaflets that students have been looking at.

Homework

Ask students to find a text about growing up to bring to the next lesson. At this stage, you should be able to ask them to work in pairs and list the key points of their texts to share in the next lesson. Ask them to be prepared to report on **two** areas: key ideas and two examples of information that needs close reading.

Answers

Activity 1
3 a pepperoni and minced beef.
   b spicy chilli.
   c mozzarella cheese, three cheeses, cheese crust.

Activity 2
2 Lemon, banana and strawberry.
3 Peanut butter and coconut.

Activity 3
2 Any two of: vanilla, chocolate, banana, lemon.
3 a van milk chocolate.
   b vanilla.
   c vanilla or chocolate.

Reading lesson plans

Student book pages 16–17

4 Reading closely for detailed understanding

Aim
- Read a text closely to understand texts in detail.

Lesson learning and objectives
- Use close reading to find and understand details in a text.

Lesson starter: individual/pair work

Direct students to the 'This lesson will help you' and the Watch out! boxes on page 16 of the student book. Link the point about reading the question carefully with the importance of finding key words in tasks and questions as identified in the previous lesson.

Ask pairs to read question 2a only of **Activity 1** and then scan Text A. Take class feedback. Ask students what they looked for as they scanned the text. Responses should include, for example, looking for anywhere where they could see '21'. Ask the class how long it took them to find the answer, and what the answer is.

Main teaching and learning

Ask pairs or small groups to look at Activity 1, question 2b, c and d. Take feedback. Discuss with the class how they read the text to arive at their answers.

Take students through question 3. Establish that this task requires them to read the text closely. As far as possible, draw this out from the students rather than giving them the 'answer.' Direct pairs to carry out three activities:
1 Look at what the students say.
2 Go back to the text and read closely.
3 Identify any mistakes and correct them.

Ask students who worked together on the previous lesson's homework task to present their chosen text. Ask them to report on key ideas and to provide two examples of information that needed close reading.

Plenary

Either record students' responses to the following questions on the whiteboard, **or** provide A3 paper and ask them to record and share their responses. Ask: What are your mistakes? How have you corrected them? In what two ways have you had to read the texts in this lesson to complete the tasks?

Homework

Ask students to go through Text A on page 17 of the student book and write a list of the main points in each paragraph.

Answers

Activity 1
2 a lines 1–3
   b lines 4–6
   c lines 9–11
   d lines 4–5, 7–9 and 12–13

3
- In the USA you can vote once you are 21.
- In India you have to be 18 to marry if you are female.
- In the UK you can marry at 16. You must be 18 to vote, gamble, drink and smoke.
- Most teenagers think their 18th is the bigger of the two.
- 'But 21 is your chance to celebrate adulthood...'
- Many 19–20-year-olds think that 21 is the biggest deal.

Reading lesson plans

Student book pages 18–19

5 Identifying the main point in a paragraph

Aim
- Identify the main points and ideas and how they are presented in a variety of texts.

Lesson learning and objectives
- Identify the main point in a paragraph. Explain what the main ideas are in a text.

Lesson starter: individual/pair work

Take students back to Text A on page 17 of the student book. In pairs, ask them to share their homework activity ideas about the main point in each paragraph. Link this activity with their own writing – how a paragraph takes a main point and develops it. Take class feedback to ensure understanding.

Expand on the Watch out! box on page 18 of the student book to reiterate that copying directly from the text does not show understanding and will not be rewarded.

Ask pairs to read Text A on page 18 and answer question 2, **Activity 1**. Discuss the main ideas of Text A as a class.

Main teaching and learning

Draw students' attention to question 3 of **Activity 1** as an example of a multiple-choice question. In pairs, ask students to decide the answer to the question and discuss how they made their choice. In class feedback, encourage students to discuss how they arrived at the answer, including the grounds on which they dismissed some distractors and any problems they had choosing between two likely answers. Elicit from the students the importance of reading the choices closely.

Direct pairs to decide on the tradition described in the second paragraph of Text A. Emphasise that they need to read the whole paragraph, as a heading gives only a partial answer and is intended to structure writing and generate interest.

Direct students to **Activity 2** on page 19 and ask them to read Text B, or read it to them if they need support. Question 2 is another example of a multiple choice. Encourage students to read the question closely and elicit from them that the key word in the question is 'main.'

In pairs, ask students to discuss and answer question 3.

Plenary

Discuss the order of the points made in Text B and ask students how they decided on the order. Explain that in writing we sequence our ideas, and as readers the students have read and recognised the sequence in this text. Reiterate that the main ideas are to be found in each paragraph. This will reinforce the function of paragraphing in reading as well as in students' own writing.

Homework

Ask students to bring in a text (article/leaflet etc.) promoting a tour, e.g. a sightseeing, entertainment or sports tour.

Answers

Activity 1
3 C
4 The tradition described is kidnapping the bride before her wedding day. Whoever finds her from the groom's family will then marry within a year.

Activity 2
2 B
3 C, B, A

Student book pages 20–21

Reading lesson plans

6 Understanding main points and ideas

Aim
- Identify the main points and ideas and how they are presented in a variety of texts.

Lesson learning and objectives
- Find and understand a text's main ideas.

Lesson starter: individual/pair work

Remind students that the features of texts include headings, pictures and captions. Link back to reading strategies previously used. Remind students that they will be looking at each paragraph in turn and use this opportunity to reinforce the importance and the function of paragraphing.

Select a suitable tour leaflet/article from the previous lesson's homework task and either display using light pro and whiteboard or duplicate for one copy between two students.

Ask students to decide:
1. The main idea of the text.
2. What the first two paragraphs are about.

Take feedback through class discussion. If the Starter activity was successful, you could engage in a brief second Starter activity before moving on to the main teaching and learning: ask pairs to show each other their homework leaflet examples. Ask them to briefly consider the main idea and how paragraphing is used. Take feedback through class discussion.

Main teaching and learning

Direct pairs or small groups to look at Text A on page 21 of the student book. If possible, distribute A3 copies of Text A so that students can highlight/annotate as they go through the tasks. Read the text with them to ensure that they are not confused by 'vinspired' presented as a word. Direct students to read question 2 of **Activity 1** and discuss what the text is about. Point out the advice in the Watch out! box on page 20. In feedback, encourage them to refer to the features when discussing what they consider to be the main idea of the whole text.

Ask small groups **either** to look at each part of question 3, complete it and feed back as a class before moving on to the next, **or** direct them to look at a and b, feed back as a class, and then move on to c and d.

When the students feed back, ask them to identify the relevant section of the text and how they used features to help them provide their answers.

Ask students to summarise the key messages of each paragraph to reinforce their learning of how texts and paragraphs work.

Plenary

Discuss the key messages of each paragraph. Students may refer to some of the following points and/or give some valid suggestions of their own: 'bigvbus' is eye-catching/targets 16–25-year-olds/caters for special access requirements/is eco-friendly.'

Concluding comments should involve relating what students have done in this lesson to being functional readers, and how these skills are essential when we need to access information in a text. You could ask them to think of examples of when they have needed to do this.

Homework

Ask students to write up the main idea of Text A from page 21 of the student book and key messages of each paragraph in their exercise book/files.

Answers

Activity 1
2. The main idea of the whole text is to use a bus at all the major festivals to recruit volunteers aged 16–25.
3. a The bigvbus is going on tour to inspire young people to do some good.
   b A team of volunteers is needed to join the event and film production team to recruit more volunteers.
   c Visitors will be able to watch films, talk to staff and/or sign up for one of the vinspired film workshops to see how professional films are made.
   d The main idea of describing the green credentials is to show that the bus meets low emission targets and to encourage people to follow their example and be green.

Reading lesson plans

Student book pages 22–23

7 Identifying details

Aim
- Read and understand texts in detail.

Lesson learning and objectives
- Identify details in a text.

Lesson starter: individual/pair work

Take students through the introduction on page 22 of the student book. Emphasise that this guidance is good to refer to when reading for detail and will also be a helpful revision tool.

Read Text A with the class. Ask pairs or threes to decide what features suggest that it is a web page. Take class feedback, encouraging students to make links between what makes it a web page and the features identified. (This will link with lessons 9 and 10.)

Main teaching and learning

Direct pairs to work on questions 2a and 2b of **Activity 1** and then feed back as a whole class discussion. Encourage students to share the detail from the text and to recognise this as an essential part of being a functional reader: point out the advice in the Top tip box on page 22.

Ask students to complete all of question 3, finding out about 'day 1' using the strategies applied in question 2. Take feedback as a class discussion.

Carry out a similar exercise for question 4 and take feedback as a class discussion.

Read the postcard with the class and point out that the use of the word 'wonderful' in the text is not giving them the answers for the postcard regarding 'wonderful' things that they have seen.

Give students copies of the blank postcard and ask them to answer question 5 as an individual activity. Ask students to share their answers to complete the postcard as a class discussion. Encourage students to support all ideas with evidence from the text.

As an additional activity, ask small groups to look at each of the three sections (Trip description, Day 1 and Day 2). Give each group an A3 copy of the text and ask them to underline/highlight details for each paragraph.

Plenary

Discuss the details of each section, looking at how students have identified the details and what skills they have used.

Homework

Ask students to write a postcard about day 1, based on the information in Text A, including **six** details. Provide blank copies of the postcard on page 22 so they can complete it and put it in their file. This will help to link their Reading and Writing skills.

Answers

2 a Line 5.
  b Minimum Sponsorship: £1300

3 a Lines 12–22, under the subheading Day 1: London to Portsmouth
  b 114kms/71 miles

4 breakfast on board the ferry on the way to France; a picnic lunch in the French countryside; dinner in a restaurant at Bernay.

5 We had to cycle for <u>100km/63 miles</u> on the second day but at least we got to <u>sleep</u> on the ferry from <u>Portsmouth</u> first. Two of the wonderful things we saw were <u>tiny villages/bubbling brooks/farmhouses/fields of horses/medieval buildings/remains of mills</u>. We stayed the night in Bernay, which has a famous <u>Benedictine</u> abbey.

Student book pages 24–25

8 Understanding texts in detail

Aim
- Read and understand texts in detail. Utilise information contained in texts.

Lesson learning and objectives
- Understand the main points and the details in a text.

Lesson starter: individual/pair work

Share the learning objective and emphasise that finding appropriate detail is part of being a functional reader. Take students through the strategies listed at the top of page 24 of the student book, and point out that they are also useful as a revision tool.

Ask pairs to identify the features of Text A. Make sure they can support their answers by referring to features and purpose.

Take feedback through class discussion and draw out uses of captions, heading, pictures, quotation and paragraphs. Highlight the use of holly to show the text is something to do with Christmas. Read the whole of Text A with the class.

Main teaching and learning

In pairs, students answer question 2 of **Activity 1**. Explain that they only need to write the facts in note form (not sentences) and that they need three points to answer the question fully. Students answer question 3 individually so that they are confident in responding to a question independently. Take class feedback.

Pairs answer question 4; remind them of the strategies they need to use to answer a multiple-choice question. During feedback, go through each distractor and discuss why it might/might not be the correct answer.

Activity 2 is a good opportunity for close-reading the text. Ask students whether or not they agree with the two responses in the speech bubbles and discuss their views and the Watch out! box on page 24 before moving on to the next aspect of the task. Ask which view they think is the most accurate.

Small groups find details in Text A to support their views. Ask them to discuss the evidence in the text and then list the details about the Crisis Centre. Use this small group discussion as a Speaking, listening and communication opportunity and share this connection with the students.

Plenary

As a class, discuss the details taken from Text A and stress that the need to be able to read closely for detail is an important life skill.

Homework

Ask students to list their thoughts about how Text A is presented.

Answers

Activity 1

2 Answers could include any three of the following:
- £50 could enable two homeless people to learn new skills.
- 144 guests wrote CVs and job applications last Christmas.
- Crisis centres are open at Christmas to allow homeless, unemployed people to create CVs and develop skills that enable them to get a job.
- Crisis centres have a library and an IT suite.
- Crisis centres offer housing advice.

3 Answers could include any two of the following:
- Crisis offers guests services which enable them to improve their English and maths.
- Crisis has a well-equipped IT centre where guests can create their CVs which will help them to kick-start their careers.
- Guests can use the IT facilities to contact friends and family.

4 A and D.

Activity 2

2 I disagree with the first speech bubble as the centres offer housing advice to help people find and keep accommodation so therefore people are not completely sent back to the streets. It is also not cruel as it allows them to be independent rather than being reliant on somebody else. It is therefore not a waste as the money offers these people a chance to change. I agree with the second speech bubble as the centre clearly offers the guests enough opportunities to turn their lives around and therefore change.

Reading lesson plans

Student book pages 26–27

⑨ Identifying how texts are presented

Aim
- Identify how the main points and ideas are presented in a variety of texts.

Lesson learning and objectives
- Identify the different presentation features used in a text. Understand why they are used.

Lesson starter: individual/pair work

Remind students of their work in the previous lesson and ask them to discuss the features of Text A on page 25. Explain how this leads into the current lesson and draw their attention to the Watch out! box – they need to work out *why* a presentational feature has been used. Also share and discuss the strategies and reinforce their value. In particular, draw students' attention to the question they have been told to ask themselves: How does this feature help the writer to convey their ideas to their readers? Encourage students to look more objectively at how a text is constructed and the possible reasons/purpose. Make links between this and students' own writing in Functional English, which has purpose and audience.

Ask pairs to work through **Activity 1**, question 2, making links between the features and the different text types. Take feedback through class discussion. Take the opportunity to encourage students to look at the purpose of a particular text type.

Main teaching and learning

Direct small groups to discuss all of Activity 1 question 3, linking each answer with the features of the text identified. Each subtask considers how the feature may help the reader – direct groups to think about *why* a feature may have been used. Give a few minutes for each task followed by feedback, so that this part of the lesson falls into four sections as per the questions. Discuss any points arising from these four activities.

Small groups revisit each text and comment on its features and presentation. Direct students to make some notes as they discuss the texts, as there will be homework arising from this activity.

Plenary

Discuss each text again and summarise the presentation and features that make each a particular text type.

Homework

Write about how each text is presented, using ideas shared during the lesson.

Answers

Activity 1

2 Text A is an email. Text B is a poster and Text C is an advert.

3 a Text C has a heading. This helps readers to clearly see what subject the advert is related to.
  b Text A. This might be useful as it provides a direct link to the article and avoids confusion for readers if they have to look for the link.
  c Text B has an image to show customers what they are buying and to entice other potential buyers.
  d The chart shows the figures in an easy to read format.

Reading lesson plans

Student book pages 28–29

10 Understanding how texts are presented

Aim
- Read and understand texts in detail. Identify the main points and ideas and how they are presented in a variety of texts.

Lesson learning and objectives
- Understand presentation features. Explain what effect they have on readers.

Lesson starter: individual/pair work

Use the homework set in the previous lesson as an introductory discussion for this lesson and to reinforce what was learned in the previous lesson. Share the strategies (and the Top tip box) with students, explaining that they now need to show their understanding of why a particular text is presented using specified features.

Read Text A with the class. Look at question 2 of **Activity 1** and remind students that they will be asked a question about the main purpose of a text in the examination.

Pairs decide what is the main purpose of Text A. Remind them of the strategies they need to use to select the correct answer from the distractors in the multiple-choice question.

Discuss the answer in feedback and ask students how they discounted the other distractors. As before, look at each distractor and discuss why it is not the correct answer.

Main teaching and learning

Take students through question 3, reading through the Feature/What/How stages of table with them to ensure that they know what they need to do and that they understand the sample answers provided. Talk to the students about how useful it can be to record information in a table (linking with Lesson 11).

In pairs, students answer question 3a. Emphasise that being able to explain *how* shows understanding. If possible, provide students with copies of the table from Activity 1 so that they do not spend lesson time copying it out. Pairs may need help finding other presentation features.

Direct pairs to join up with another pair and exchange ideas before the Plenary, making modifications to their tables where necessary.

Plenary

Discuss as a class questions 3b, 3c, and 3d and students' answers from their pair and group work. Highlight the link with their Speaking, listening and communication skills so that they recognise the value of sharing ideas and being able to express them in a discussion.

Discuss how to move from simply identifying features to showing understanding of *how* they are used. Motivate students by showing how they are making progress.

Homework

Ask students to find their own text and identify one feature, what it makes the reader notice and how it helps the text achieve its purpose.

Answers

Activity 1
2 D
3 a

Presentation feature	What does it make readers notice?	How does this help the text to achieve its purpose?
Paragraphs	They help the reader to notice the information as it is separated.	The text becomes more obvious and people are more likely to read it.
Colour	Bold red/white heading.	Grabs the reader's attention.
Images	It makes the reader notice the activity being described and the audience more clearly.	People want to find out what the pictures show.

Reading lesson plans

Student book pages 30–31

Finding information in tables

Aim
- Read, understand and utilise information contained in tables.

Lesson learning and objectives
- Find and use information presented in tables.

Lesson starter: individual/pair work

Ask students to share their homework examples set in the previous lesson. If possible, make links with information in tables and remind students how the table in the previous lesson helped to present information and ideas more clearly. Then ask pairs to briefly list examples of information they have seen set out as a table. Take feedback in class discussion.

Read through the Top tip box on page 30 of the student book and point out two different ways in which students will use reading skills they have practised in previous lessons. Take them through the strategies for finding information in tables and reinforce the value of these strategies, both in the real world and as a useful revision tool.

Main teaching and learning

Read all of the text in **Activity 1** with the students. If possible, make copies of Tables A and B and stick them on A3 paper so that students can annotate/highlight them. These could later be displayed for revision purposes. Pairs work through question 2. Ask them to discuss how they are using their reading skills to find information. Take feedback in class discussion: talk about the functionality of the task as well as going through the answers for question 2. Focus on the structure of the table and ask students what features are used to present the information.

Read all the text for **Activity 2** with your students. Direct pairs to find the information needed to answer questions 2, 3 and 4 by looking at Table B. Take feedback in a class discussion.

Explain that **Activity 3** is an example of where students can apply their understanding of how to use information in realistic scenarios. Read the three paragraphs about Kerri, Ashley and Mo to the students.

Direct small groups to answer question 3. Make sure that they can give reasons for their decisions. They might choose much earlier trains to allow extra time.

If you have time, ask groups to set up a different scenario or respond to one provided by you as an extra task, e.g. which train should Sam catch if she wants to travel from Birchwood to Warrington and be there by 8.40 a.m.?

Plenary

Take feedback in a class discussion. Ask students to discuss the importance of being able to use and understand tables in real-life situations, e.g. Ashley might have missed a job opportunity if he had not read the timetable correctly.

Homework

Ask students to find an example of a different type of table to keep in their file/book. Ask them to note the type and purpose of the information in the table they have chosen in their file/book.

Answers

Activity 1
2 a 1995
  b Craig T Nelson, Holly Hunter, Samuel L Jackson and Jason Lee.
  c *Finding Nemo*
  d *Amélie* and *Monty Python's Life of Brian*.
  e *Shrek* and *Amélie*.

Activity 2
2 6.22 a.m.   3 6.45 a.m.   4 4

Activity 3
3
- Kerri should catch the train that leaves Birchwood at 8.24 a.m. and arrives at Liverpool Lime Street at 8.57 a.m.
- Ashley should catch the train that leaves Manchester Piccadilly at 8.37 and arrives at 8.57, but he would have to run.
- Mo should catch the train that leaves Manchester Airport at 6.41 a.m. and arrives at Birchwood at 7.24 a.m.

Reading lesson plans

Student book pages 32–33

12 Finding information in charts

Aim
- Read, understand and utilise information contained in charts.

Lesson learning and objectives
- Find and use information presented in charts.

Lesson starter: individual/pair work

Display the examples of charts on page 32 of the student book. Ask pairs to think about when they use charts; take suggestions. Draw students' attention to the need to understand text types using a chart. Students may refer to subjects such as Maths, Science and Geography, but charts are used in all sorts of contexts.

Main teaching and learning

Direct students to look at Chart A in **Activity 1** and note the information given in it.

Ask in pairs to answer question 3. Draw their attention to the fact that it is a multiple-choice question and ask them to approach it in a similar way as before. Hold a quick class discussion about which is the correct answer.

Ask students to look at the three distractors and explain why they are discounted. Ask them to look at the presentational features of Chart A and how the text uses the pie chart in the form of a plate of food. This will reinforce previous lessons about how and why texts are presented in a particular way.

Ask pairs to answer question 2 in **Activity 2**. Draw their attention to the wording 'According to the chart', and discuss what this instruction means, i.e. that their answer must be based on what is in the chart (also highlighted in the Watch out! box on page 33 of the student book. Point out that Charts A and B are both pie charts, but Chart A is more visual and uses images of food for each section.

Ask pairs to identify the chart used in **Activity 3** and list two points about popular foods based on what the chart tells them. Direct pairs to share their ideas with another pair and then take feedback as a class discussion.

Ask pairs to discuss which chart they found most helpful for finding information.

Plenary

Discuss how information is presented in a variety of ways and text types, and evaluate the user-friendliness of each of the charts.

Homework

Ask each student to find an example of a text with information in a chart and bring it to the next lesson.

Answers

Activity 1
3 C

Activity 2
2 C

Activity 3
2 Answers might include:
- Fish and chips are the least popular type of fast food.
- Pizza is the most popular type of fast food.

© Pearson Education Limited 2010

Reading lesson plans

Student book pages 34–35

13 Reading a text and responding to it

Aim
- Read and understand texts in detail. Identify suitable responses to texts.

Lesson learning and objectives
- Decide how to respond to a text.

Lesson starter: individual/pair work

Share charts brought in from the previous lesson's homework task. Remind students about Lesson 11, where they were asked to use the timetable to find trains for Kerri, Ashley and Mo. Link this with the idea that we not only need to read and understand texts, but that there are also times when we need to respond to what we have read.

Take students through the learning objective and the strategies on page 34 of the student book. Draw their attention to the Top tip box about the number of marks and the answer space providing clues about how much needs to be written.

Ask pairs to decide what is the main purpose of Text A, giving a reason for their answer.

Main teaching and learning

Ask pairs to answer questions 2, 3 and 4 of **Activity 1**, then share their answers with another pair. Discuss the answers to the questions as a whole class. Ask students to locate the relevant part of the text that gave them the answer. In small groups, look again at Text A and identify presentational features. Share ideas through class discussion.

Ask students to look at **Activity 2** and decide what is the main purpose of Text B. This is usually printed on a plastic bag that is posted through the householder's letter box – if possible, bring in an example. Ask pairs to look at presentational features of the text and feed back to the class. Pairs answer questions 2 and 3 and feed back in class discussion. Draw students' attention to the number of things required in the question, i.e. three. Use this as an opportunity to reinforce the importance of understanding the precise demands of the question and looking at the number of marks allocated to it.

Plenary

Share the three things required as a response to the NSPCC instructions. Look at how we are often required to respond to something that we have read and link this with the L1 Reading skill standard and coverage and range.

Homework

Ask students to find a similar text to Text B and note its main purpose and the actions or responses needed.

Answers

Activity 1

2 The parcel is currently at the Royal Mail Delivery Office in Walton-On-Thames.

3 To collect the parcel I will have to bring the collection card and a form of identification to the Delivery Office where I can then collect my package between 7.30 a.m. and 1 p.m.

4 If I wanted to have the parcel redelivered I would have to call the Delivery Office or go to the company website and request redelivery.

Activity 2

2 The NSPCC want me to support them by giving good-quality clothes, shoes and textiles which can be collected between 8 a.m. and 7 p.m. in a bag provided to help Clothes Aid.

3 I have to make sure that they are good quality, can be collected between 8 a.m. and 7 p.m., and that I only donate clothes, shoes or other textiles.

Approaches to teaching Speaking, listening and communication

Students are assessed in two separate but related areas: formal discussion and informal discussion. The two areas must be designated for assessment purposes rather than as 'opportunistic' assessments. This is a requirement for Functional English assessment, but also emphasises the importance of this component in terms of your students being functional users of English in all the language modes.

Introduction

Use the introductory pages to this section to share the skills standards, aims and areas of assessments with your students. As soon as possible, take them through the assessment grids which are drawn from the criteria to reinforce what is expected of them when they are assessed in this component. The student book contains materials for the two lessons and each section covers the different types of discussion needed, including how they should prepare for Speaking, listening and communication in carefully managed stages.

The lessons

Use pair/group activities in the Reading and Writing lessons as opportunities to develop Speaking, listening and communication skills. Share this with the students by reassuring them that they are using their speaking, listening and communication skills in discussions related to their reading and writing so that they can grow in confidence in this component through their pair/group work. Discuss with the students the types of contexts for each discussion and link with the texts and related reading and writing activities in terms of functionality. Their discussions must be grounded in reality/real-life contexts as exemplified in the student book. Ensure that students have established an understanding of the differences between formal and informal discussion. They will do so through the activities in the student book/lesson plans where their preparations are through individual work and in discussions with their peers. For both types of discussion, preparation is essential.

Participation in discussions

Use the activities in the student book where students research a topic and think of questions to ask/ contributions to make in discussions.

Through their preparations for the assessments, direct students to ensure that:

- their contributions to discussions are relevant and extended where this is appropriate
- they allow for the input of others and respond to their contributions showing that they have been listening by beginning 'the point you just made about...'
- they prepare fully, researching and recording ideas for contributions
- they have something to contribute in both formal and informal discussions of ideas and opinions
- they prepare to make different kinds of contributions such as a question for clarification, a comment, a particular role such as chairing a discussion, interviewer, interviewee
- they present information and ideas clearly
- their body language is positive – good eye contact, facing those in discussion and avoiding folding arms, gazing into space or reading/writing if this is not part of the activity
- they use appropriate language – use Reading and Writing lessons to reinforce the importance of form, tone, audience.

Wherever possible, emphasise that these are life skills we need to function successfully in real-life situations where it is essential that we demonstrate speaking, listening and communication skills and related, positive behaviours.

It is important that students understand the differences between formal and informal discussions. Elicit from students how both require preparation, turn-taking, questions, contributions, bringing others into the discussion and using questions to move the discussion forward. Discuss with students the specific roles that are required in formal discussions, such as chairing a discussion, and how there is usually an agenda and an outcome such as reaching a decision.

You might want to take some of these areas and target them for further development. For example, encourage students to think about the questions that they ask and how to revisit points. Through pair/group work, the students could list different ways to contribute in response to the views and opinions of others. At Level 1, students are assessed regarding allowing others to provide input and then responding appropriately. They could construct the types of phrases/sentences that could be used to develop/demonstrate the ability to allow the contributions of others and make their own responses. Students could record their ideas and display them on posters to reinforce their learning and for revision purposes. They could also design display posters to show:

1 How an agenda is constructed
2 The different roles in a discussion
3 Identification of the features of formal and informal discussions.

Additional points

Emphasise the importance of:
- using notes as prompts only; they should resist using them as scripts
- demonstrating good listening skills in follow up questions/comments
- expressing their own views, ideas, opinions and balancing these with listening to others and demonstrating respect for their contributions.

Reinforce the different aspects of this component. Speaking is active participation, follow-up questions/comments show that they have participated as a listener and body language and other non-verbal communications are also important parts of the communication process.

Using these different approaches and making links with functionality in reading and writing, should help your students to become confident in their application of Speaking, listening and communication skills and appreciate the importance of applying them not only for assessment purposes but also beyond this in real-life situations.

Speaking, listening and communication lesson plans

Student book pages 46–49

Taking part in an informal discussion

Aim
- Make relevant and extended contributions to informal discussion, allowing for and responding to others' input.
- Present information/points of view clearly and in appropriate language.

Lesson learning and objectives
- Take part in an informal discussion. Make clear, relevant contributions. Listen to others.

Lesson starter: individual/pair work

Take students through the guidance on page 44 of the student book and link it with the skill standard on page 45. Remind them to think about the skill standard when preparing for Speaking, listening and communication, including before and during discussions, as well as those that take place in Reading and Writing lessons.

Take students through the guidance (including the Watch out! box) on page 46. Discuss the task and direct pairs to look at the key skills needed for successful discussions. Discuss these skills as a class.

Direct pairs to **Activity 1**, question 1. Ask them to share their ideas with another pair before feeding back to the whole class.

Main teaching and learning

Direct students to choose two points from their list and plan how to explain these points fully. One point will be used in the group discussion and the other in 'Step 2 Active listening'. Direct students to explain their points to a partner.

During **Activity 2**, groups use the assessment grid on page 47 of the student book; this is a good use of the opportunity to self- and peer-assess. Show students the assessment grid from the Specification.

Share the peer feedback with the whole class. Rather than name peers, ask each group to share examples of good discussion contributions and areas that need development.

Take students through the Step 2 Active listening guidance on page 47 of the student book. This time, look at how well the groups listen, using the grid for peer- and self-assessment on page 47. Share feedback as before, so that only the good practice and areas for improvement are identified, rather than identifying individuals.

Small groups discuss the contributions from Groups A, B and C in **Activity 3**. Which are effective? Which need more work? Take class feedback.

Draw students' attention to the Top tip box on page 48 and make sure they recognise this as a tool to involve others and move the discussion forward.

Take students through the guidance on page 49 and instruct them to complete **Activity 4**. After their discussion, ask them to carry out their self-assessment, then get them to share it with a partner. Encourage students to be positive and constructive in their assessments of each other.

Ask groups to share key messages and things they have learnt about taking part in a discussion. Direct students to make notes of their views in preparation for the Plenary. These will also act as reference notes for future discussion work, so students need to be aware of their importance.

Plenary

Discuss the outcome of the self-assessments and the key messages/what students have learned during the lesson. Ask students what went well and what needs more work, and ask them to record one positive point and one requiring more work.

Homework

Ask students to look at a topic that interests them that they could use as the basis for a discussion. If time allows, you could give them opportunities during a lesson for research on their chosen topic, and ask them to identify six points for discussion as work outside the lesson. This could lead to further practice discussions in preparation for the assessment itself.

Speaking, listening and communication lesson plans

Student book pages 50–53

2 Taking part in a formal discussion

Aim
- Prepare for and contribute to the formal discussion of ideas and opinions.
- Make different kinds of contributions to discussions.
- Present information/points of view clearly and in appropriate language.

Lesson learning and objectives
- Prepare for a formal discussion and using appropriate language, adopting different roles.

Lesson starter: individual/pair work

Ask small groups to discuss the following:
1. What were the key messages/things learned in the previous lesson?
2. What did you learn about taking part in an informal discussion?
3. What do you think are the differences between formal and informal discussion?

Discuss their thoughts as a whole class, including the Top tip box on page 50.

Talk about what it means to adopt different roles, ensuring that students are not confusing the idea of the role of a chair with a dramatic role.

Read the topic set on page 50 with students, then go through Step 1. It is important to discuss the role of the chair. Refer back to Activity 3 on page 48, which shows examples of participants moving the discussion on and involving others.

Provide students with an example of an agenda so they know what it looks like. They need to understand what the term means and what is expected of them.

Main teaching and learning

Students work through all of **Activity 1**. For question 4, you might want to introduce the idea of 'counter-argument', but this depends on your students. Take class feedback, asking students to share their reasons for choosing their charity and not choosing other charities.

Take students through the Top tip box on page 52. Draw their attention to the Step 2 guidance and encourage them to use this as a checklist for their discussions.

Direct students to carry out the tasks in **Activity 2**. Take feedback for the two points made in support of the charity, two points in response to other people's suggestions and how helpful they found each other's feedback.

Recap the 'Chairing a discussion' section. Small groups work through **Activity 3**. Get them to swap roles every few minutes so that all have the opportunity to chair the meeting. Take feedback if there is time.

Direct groups to Step 3 and ask them to create the agenda. Discuss with them how an agenda makes the discussion formal.

For **Activity 4** the students have the discussion. The student book gives 10 minutes for this activity and it is not recommended to go beyond this time. The chair needs to end it and sum up any decisions. Students need to make a note of these decisions for reporting back in the Plenary.

Ask students to assess their skills on their own using the self-assessment checklist in Step 5. You may want to provide copies so that students can annotate it with their thoughts on how well they have done.

Direct students to share their self-assessment with a partner and discuss the skills they feel confident about and any areas that need developing.

Plenary

Discuss self-assessments as a class. Ask the chair and other members of the group to give their decision on the chosen charity and how they reached that decision.

Sum up the activities. What helped the discussion to flow?

Homework

Ask students to research topics that could be used in a formal discussion assessment and work on preparing points for a discussion with a partner.

Approaches to teaching Writing

Introduction

The Writing section of the student book provides opportunities for students to practise their writing skills using a variety of functional, real-life contexts. The activities across the thirteen sections are designed to help students to develop skills that are transferable to different situations where writing is required and equip them with the tools they need to be functional writers at Level 1.

It would be useful to take students through the introductory pages of the Writing section as they set out areas for assessment, the aims required and give an overview of the learning experiences provided.

The lessons and the sample assessment materials, including the mark schemes, all contribute to the understanding that students need to have of what it means to be functional writers and how they can get to this stage themselves.

The lessons

Lesson plans have been derived from each part of the writing section for you to deliver to your students. The lessons:
- address each aspect of the aims
- go through the different forms of writing
- provide practise opportunities in manageable sections leading to complete writing tasks
- contextualise technical aspects of writing such as spelling and punctuation.

Encourage students to establish links with other Writing and Reading lessons, using the texts as models for their own writing. The texts are forms which students are expected to adopt in their own writing according to purpose and audience.

Modelling writing skills

Use an OHP/digital projector or simply a whiteboard to take students through your thought processes as you construct a piece of writing. The National Literacy Strategy offers some useful resources, including helpful scaffolding techniques such as writing and thinking frames, so that students have support as they write. As you model some writing, you could encourage students to discuss their own thought processes when they write. Providing mini-whiteboards will encourage students to experiment with their own writing, using your examples as a starting point.

Planning their writing

It is vital that students plan their writing: emphasise how important this is. Experience shows that some students are reluctant to plan, perhaps regarding it as a low priority. The lesson plans provide opportunities for students to plan their responses in varying degrees of detail and for a range of contexts. There are also many activities where students share their planning/ideas with a partner or group and in class discussions. Peer review is often recommended, as reviewing gives the planning more of a status.

Discuss with students the importance of planning and elicit from them such points as:
- it gives writing a structure
- it helps them sustain the appropriate form
- it helps them to think of style/purpose/audience.

You may want to share 'expert feedback', such as examiner reports, with students where concerns about lack of planning are often expressed.

Technical aspects of writing

Throughout the student book, opportunities to practise spelling, punctuation and grammar are presented in contextualised activities. For each aspect being targeted there is exemplification which in itself is useful as a checklist/revision tool. There are also activities related to each aspect which allow students to engage actively. Contextualising a particular technical aspect of language allows you to teach the application of skills so that students relate what they have learned to their own writing. Teaching technical aspects in this way enables students to understand the relevance of this to their own writing. To show the importance of technical accuracy, you could draw their attention to the 40% minimum weighting that this has when their writing is assessed.

Use of a dictionary

Encourage students to use a dictionary in the following situations:
- looking up the meanings of key words in the Functional Skills Criteria
- looking up meanings of words in reading texts and writing stimulus
- looking up meanings of words in questions
- when preparing for writing tasks as presented in the student book, particularly in the sections focusing on technical skills.

Writing lesson plans

There are many ways to use dictionaries in your lessons. You could enhance suggested starter activities by providing words for students to look up in their dictionaries, or you could give them the word verbally and ask students to look for the spelling. Another supporting activity could take the form of posters, with students writing instructions of how to use a dictionary, complete with annotated exemplification.

The prospect of accessing and using a dictionary may be daunting for some Level 1 learners so you may wish to restrict early activities to locating a few words at a time, perhaps working sequentially so that they become familiar with the alphabet and can apply this knowledge to the use of a dictionary.

Resources/further teaching ideas

Many of the lesson plans contain recommendations regarding photocopying a task/activity to enable collaborative work and active learning. Annotated/highlighted texts reinforce learning, provide resources for display and serve as a revision resource.

Encourage students to measure their writing alongside a 'checklist' – the self-assessment grids may be useful here. Students should ask themselves the following types of questions:
- Have I written clearly?
- Have I used enough detail?
- Have I set out my ideas/information in a logical sequence?
- Have I written for the right audience?
- Have I a clear sense of purpose?
- Have I used the right form?
- Have I used sentences?
- Have I checked my spelling?

You might elicit such a list from students themselves and lead this into their production of posters that could be used to reinforce learning and act as prompts in writing tasks.

All the sections are useful to focus students on particular aspects of their writing, and they are also an excellent revision resource. The section on understanding of form, for example, is something that students could return to again and again as the texts are useful examples of particular types with supporting comments provided in the call-out boxes.

For further opportunities to teach students through active engagement with different writing forms, when you ask students to identify forms, you could develop this further.

Ask students to identify different writing forms that they might expect to find, and either use examples from the Reading and Writing sections of the student book and/or direct them to find their own examples to display with annotations showing:
- form
- audience
- style
- purpose.

Also include features that make this piece of writing a particular text type.

As with Speaking, listening and communication, reinforce at all times how the writing skills that students are acquiring and developing throughout this course have a direct relevance to the world beyond the classroom and have real-life applications. You might want to discuss employability with your students and how the ability to write clearly, appropriately and accurately is highly valued.

Writing for your audience

Student book pages 62–63

Aim
- Use language, format and structure suitable for the audience.

Lesson learning and objectives
- Suit your writing to your audience.

Lesson starter: individual/pair work

Discuss the guidance on page 62 of the student book and link it with the Reading section where an understanding of audience was established.

Share the learning objective and the Top tip box on page 62. Read question 1, **Activity 1**. Write the following questions on a whiteboard/flip chart and ask small groups to consider them:
- To whom is the letter being addressed?
- What is the subject?
- What sort of language needs to be used?

Take class feedback.

Main teaching and learning

Talk students through question 2, Activity 1. Direct them to individually make notes for the task. Ask pairs to share their ideas and discuss similarities/differences in their approach, then share their ideas with the rest of the class. Get them to think about effective notes and how they are forming the basis of a plan for a draft of this task.

Pairs then decide the audience for each of Tasks A, B and C in **Activity 2**. Ask students to decide on the audience for each task and to consider the purpose. Share ideas with another pair before taking class feedback.

Students to complete question 2 individually, then share with a partner. If students use plain A4/A3 paper, their work could be displayed for revision purposes.

Discuss question 3 with students. They may argue that both B and C are letters and so need to be written in an agreed form. (See Lesson 3 on page 45.)

It is useful to discuss the need for clear English in all tasks, even if some are more formal than others.

Pairs complete questions 1 to 4 in **Activity 3**, and make notes for the plenary. Individually, students complete question 5, then share their paragraphs with a partner and discuss strengths/areas for development.

Plenary

Discuss students' thoughts on the different student versions in Activity 3 and on their own writing. Recap what has been learned in this lesson.

Homework

Direct students to write the opening paragraph of the letter to the MP. Discuss the sort of language they need to use and what the MP needs to know so that they are clear what is required for the task.

Answers

Activity 1
1 The local council.

3 Use a letter format to ensure it looks professional; use paragraphs to separate the text; use connectives to link points together.

Activity 2
1 Task A: drivers; Task B: your MP; Task C: the council.

2 The audience needs to know about accidents that have happened while drivers have been using mobiles; headsets that can be used instead of mobiles; possible advantages of driving while talking on a hands-free phone (e.g. keeps drivers awake on long journeys).

3 B and C.

Activity 3
2 The audience needs to know why bins need to be emptied once a week and the repercussions if this doesn't happen.

3 Formal standard English. It should also be persuasive and include modal verbs.

4 The first paragraph is the best as it uses formal language, accurate facts and develops each point. The second paragraph demonstrates limited knowledge and does not explain anything.

Writing lesson plans

Student book pages 64–67

2 Writing to suit a purpose

Aim
- Use language, format and structure suitable for the purpose.

Lesson learning and objectives
- Suit your writing to your purpose.

Lesson starter: individual/pair work

Share the learning objective and the Watch out! box on page 64 with the class and remind them that purpose and audience go together. Ask some students to share the opening paragraphs of their letters to the MP as per the previous lesson's homework.

Draw their attention to the thought bubbles in the student book. Explain that these questions are useful when thinking about purpose, and remind students to refer to these questions whenever they are thinking about the purpose of their writing.

In pairs, students work through **Activity 1**, making a note of their ideas. Feed back and discuss as a class.

Main teaching and learning

Ask students to complete **Activity 2** and make notes for a class discussion. Get a range of responses from the class for each of the areas discussed.

Small groups to complete **Activity 3**, discussing what they should include from the student's notes in question 3 as well as their own ideas. Class feedback.

Go through the Top tip box and the Using facts and opinions guidance on page 66. Ask students to think of examples of facts and opinions, perhaps relating them to current news stories, provided that they do not cover sensitive issues.

In pairs, students complete question 1 of **Activity 1** on page 66. Feed back as a class. Individually, students complete question 2. Students to work in pairs for question 3. Ask whether they think linking fact with opinion is effective, and draw out that adding a fact makes an opinion more believable/convincing.

Individually, direct students to work through questions 1 and 2 of **Activity 2**. Students swap plans in pairs for question 3 and then share their ideas with the class.

Read Task D of **Activity 3** with students. Inform them that this will be the basis for their homework. Direct them to work through the questions, making notes about good planning, ideas, audience and purpose.

Plenary

Feedback the students' discussions for Activity 3 question 3 on page 67 as a class.

Recap on what has been learned during this lesson.

Homework

Ask students to write a first draft of their article using the plans that they have prepared in the lesson.

Answers

Activity 1
2 Task A: to inform and persuade tourists to visit places in your area. Task B: to advise and help young adults to look after their money. Task C: to persuade employers that 16- and 20-year-olds are equal and deserve the same pay.

Activity 2
2 Inform tourists about two interesting places to visit in your area.
3 Visit the two interesting places.
4 Include features of the places that will attract and interest tourists. You should use appealing language to get tourists interested.

Activity 3
2 Write a web page to advise young adults on three ways to save money.
3 B, C and E.

Using facts and opinions

Activity 1
1 A: Opinion, B: Fact, C: Fact, D: Opinion.
2 …they have no qualifications to enable them to get well-paid jobs.
3 b Opinion: 'No-one should be forced to work in a sweatshop making clothes'. This could be backed up by the fact that 1 in 10 people who work in a sweat shop will die by the time they are 40.

Student book pages 68–73

3 Understanding form

Aim
- Write clearly and coherently using appropriate form.

Lesson learning and objectives
- Choose the right form for your writing and use the right features.

Lesson starter: individual/pair work

Go through the Top tip box on page 68 with students and link references to form, features and purpose with the Reading lessons. In pairs, students read Tasks A and B of **Activity 1** and decide on their form and purpose. Students must make notes to feed back to the class.

Use class discussion to draw out what details in the task gave students information about form and purpose.

Main teaching and learning

Read Text A in **Activity 2** with students and take them through the annotations. Link 'Mr Paul Keats' with 'Yours sincerely' to reinforce correct form.

In pairs look carefully at the letter and answer question 2 of Activity 2. Pairs work through question 3. Stress the importance of using paragraphs. Ask students how Bill Bodrun uses one paragraph to state the nature of his complaint and the other to state what he wants in future.

Draw attention to the Watch out! box on page 70. Read Text B of **Activity 4** with students. Ask them to look for features that make this an article and to work through questions individually.

Go through the email and annotations in Text C of **Activity 5**. Students work through the questions and then feed back in a class discussion.

Use a similar approach with **Activity 6**, where students need to answer questions about the leaflet.

Make sure during feedback that students are clear about different forms and purposes of writing.

The student book refers to use of revision cards for **Activity 7** – a good way for students to prepare for revision and consolidate learning. You might want to supply A3 or flip chart paper.

Divide class into six groups. Each group produces a revision guide for the letter and then each group will take on the email **or** the article **or** the leaflet.

Plenary

Ask each group to show what they have produced; the rest of the class should give constructive comments.

Draw out from the students the key things that they have learned. Reinforce the advice on form given in the Top tip box on page 73, that clues may be given in the exam paper as to the form an answer should take.

Homework

Produce Task B – advice on how to use the library at your school or college.

Answers

Activity 1
2 Task A: Formal email, Task B: Informative leaflet.

Activity 2
2 a Top right hand corner, b 'Yours sincerely', c Beneath the sender's address, d On the left hand side, just above the beginning of the letter.
3 a …is about and the intentions of the writer.
   b …wants from the recipient of the letter.

Activity 4
2 a What the article is about.
   b By introducing the topic in an interesting way.
   c To bring in evidence and quotations to suppose the aim of the article.
   d It suggests that gadgets are unnecessary, backed up with a quotation.

Activity 5
2 a 'Dear [name of recipient]'.
   b Explain the background to your email.
   c By including specific details in the last few sentences.

Activity 6
2 a To clarify what it is about.
   b Introduce the topic in a general way.
   c Using paragraphs, numbered lists or sub-headings.

Writing lesson plans

Student book pages 74–77

4 Understanding style

Aim
- Ensure written work includes generally accurate punctuation and spelling and that meaning is clear.

Lesson learning and objectives
- Suit your writing style to your purpose and audience.

Lesson starter: individual/pair work

Take students through the Watch out! box on page 74 of the student book. Emphasise the importance of writing being 'fit for purpose'. Read the guidance about when to use formal and informal style and link it with formal/informal discussion, e.g. how this affects structure and tone.

Direct students to look at **Activity 1** and take them through Task A, pointing out form, audience and purpose. In pairs, students look at Tasks B, C and D, using the Task A example to help them decide the form, purpose and audience for each task. Take class feedback to check students have understood the task.

Main teaching and learning

Draw students' attention to the guidance on page 75 regarding 'Formal standard English' and 'Less formal standard English'. Point out that even where a response can be less formal, standard English should always be used. In small groups, ask students to discuss the two examples of students' writing and make a note of the differences. Ask students to share their ideas in a class discussion. Feed in the Top tip box ideas from page 76 of the student book.

In groups, students work through question 2 of **Activity 2** and then feed back to the class. Independently, students complete question 3, then share with a partner to decide if any changes need to be made. Ask students to share their writing in class discussion.

In pairs, students to complete question 2, **Activity 3**. Ask them to share their version with another pair and share some examples with the class. Individually, direct students to compose their own paragraphs for question 3 and then swap with a partner.

Take students through the explanation of apostrophe use on page 77. Ask students to complete question 2 of **Activity 4**. Then take students through the guidance on how to use apostrophes to show ownership. Discuss the common error of using apostrophes for plurals.

Individually, students work through **Activity 5** and then check each other's work in pairs.

Plenary

Draw out from students what they have learned about the two uses of the apostrophe. Emphasise that they now have a greater understanding of how to use style according to form, purpose and audience.

Answers

Activity 1
1 Task B: Form – report, Audience – the government, Purpose – to advise on what teenagers should be taught before they are 16. Task C: Form – magazine article, Audience – parents, Purpose – to discuss raising the school-leaving age to 18. Task D: Form – email, Audience – teacher, Purpose – to suggest a suitable trip for students.
2 Task A: formal, Task B: formal, Task C: informal, Task D: formal.

Activity 2
2 b The first extract.
 c Grammar is correct, no slang is used. The writing is impersonal and sensible for the topic.

Activity 3
2 b Make the language more assertive and more formal by removing the question at the end. Direct the language to the audience, not to the student.

Activity 4
2 Wouldn't, it's, don't, you'll, mustn't and aren't.

5 Planning and organising your writing

Aim
- Present information in a logical sequence.

Lesson learning and objectives
- Read writing tasks carefully to work out what you must do. Plan your texts appropriately.

Lesson starter: individual/pair work

Share the guidance and Top tip on page 78 and stress that good writing needs to be planned and organised.

Direct students to Task A, **Activity 1**. Read the context with them and the two messages on the internet discussion. In pairs, students consider whether language should be formal or informal. Ask students to make a list of the main points, ideas and details in each of the messages. Discuss the outcomes as a class, then discuss the writing task that students will need to complete individually.

Main teaching and learning

In pairs, students work through question 2. Talk about audience, purpose, form and style as a useful checklist that they could use for all writing, whether in lessons, assessments or real-life situations (job applications, etc.). In pairs, students work through questions 1 to 4 in **Activity 2**. Individually, students complete the plan and answer question 5. Direct students to swap their plan with a partner and discuss similarities, differences and areas for improvement. Feed back through class discussion.

Draw students' attention to the Top tip box on page 80. Emphasise to students that all writing needs to be organised and there are different ways to do this, depending on the form of the writing. Direct students to **Activity 3** and read Task B with the class. Remind students of their work on writing letters in Lesson 3 about form. Students work in pairs, going through the bullet points listed under the heading 'Writing task' and looking at how these give a framework to their writing. In pairs, students work through questions 2 and 3. In class feedback discuss who the letter is from and who it is going to. It may be formal, but it should appeal to parents; the style might be relaxed, but there should be no slang.

Individually, students work through **Activity 4**. Once finished, they swap with a partner and look at ways to improve their work. Students may find it useful to map their letters as on page 73 of the student book, to reinforce using correct form. Ask students to note down any points for the plenary.

Plenary

Discuss with students key things they have learned in this lesson about audience, purpose, form and style, and how important it is when planning their writing to take all of these factors into consideration.

Homework

Individually, students write their letter for Task B in final form.

Answers

Activity 1
2 a Audience: parents.
  b Purpose: to discuss whether parents should be allowed to smack their children.
  c Form: internet discussion forum message.
  d Style: informal so the parents don't feel too pressured.

Activity 3
2 a Audience: parents.
  b Purpose: to encourage children to eat more healthily and drink more water.
  c Form: a letter.
3 This letter should be written in a formal style.

Writing lesson plans

Student book pages 82–85

6 Writing in paragraphs

Aim
- Write clearly and coherently, including an appropriate level of detail. Use correct grammar, including correct and consistent use of tense.

Lesson learning and objectives
- Plan and write well-structured paragraphs. Link your paragraphs together.

Lesson starter: individual/pair work

Read the Top tip box on page 82 and the information about how to structure paragraphs with students. Emphasise that appropriate use of paragraphing is a sign of a good writer, as it shows that they know how to organise their ideas.

Make duplicate copies of Text A so students can mark where each new paragraph should begin and make annotations. In pairs, students work through **Activity 1**, question 2. Ask them to record what they think is the main point of each paragraph. Feed back in class discussion, agreeing where each new paragraph could begin and why.

Main teaching and learning

Look at the mnemonic for remembering how to construct paragraphs. In pairs, direct students to read Text B in **Activity 2** and answer questions 3, 4 and 5. In feedback make sure students are all clear which part of the paragraph gives evidence, which adds explanation and which sentence links the main point to the whole text.

Read question 2 of **Activity 3** with the class. Individually, students complete questions 3 and 4, then swap with a partner to compare. Read the linking sentence for each and discuss which is more effective and how it might be improved.

Take students through the 'Linking your ideas' section. Go through the different types of connectives with students and point out that they are useful for reference and revision. Talk the students through the questions in **Activity 4**, then ask them to complete them in pairs or small groups. Detailed class feedback.

Photocopy the paragraph in **Activity 5** so students can annotate it during their discussions on connectives. In pairs, students complete question 1 and then share their version with another pair. Feed back in class discussion.

Individually, students work through question 2 and swap with a partner to identify areas for improvement. Tell students that question 3 is their homework and get them to discuss ideas for writing.

Plenary

Discuss the paragraphs students have written and what they have learned in this lesson. The summary of paragraphing in the Top tip box on page 85 should be clearly understood by the feedback student's give you.

Talk about what sorts of things they could include in the homework task, e.g. which bands to see, what to take, travel plans, safety. How can they use what they have learned about connectives in this lesson in their own writing?

Homework

Complete question 3 of Activity 5.

Answers

Activity 1
2 A new paragraph should start after 'the latest product' and after 'so greedy'.

Activity 2
3 Evidence: 'People learn about food products through TV advertising.'
4 Explanation: 'They do not want to spend a lot of time working out what unfamiliar products to buy.'
5 Linking sentence: 'Anything that helps people to make informed decisions cannot be all bad.'

Activity 5
1 b First, so, because, in addition, so, however.

Writing lesson plans

Student book pages 86–89

7 Using main points and details

Aim
- Ensure written work includes generally accurate punctuation and spelling and that meaning is clear.

Lesson learning and objectives
- Work out the difference between a main point and detail. Use both main points and details in your paragraphs. Practise planning and writing paragraphs.

Lesson starter: individual/pair work

Share the learning objectives on page 86 with the class and make links with the previous lesson. Direct students to **Activity 1** and discuss how Text A has both a main point and details supporting that point. In pairs, direct students to work through the questions in **Activity 2**. In class discussion, ask students about both the words and the images. Explain that together they form the text.

Main teaching and learning

Read Text C of **Activity 3** with students. They should work through the questions in small groups. Divide the three questions into three separate activities, taking feedback at the end of each one before moving on.

Individually, students complete question 2 of **Activity 4**, then work with a partner to complete question 3. Ask students to share their ideas in groups and then take feedback in class discussion. Use the Watch out! box on page 88 to reinforce the message that main ideas need supporting evidence but without repetition.

Read Task A of **Activity 5** with students. Direct them in pairs to identify form, audience and purpose, and report back to class. Go through the planning table and ask students to use this to plan their paragraphs.

Individually, students complete questions 2 and 3 then invite some to share their ideas with the class. Individually, students complete question 4, then feed back in class discussion. If students have chosen the same hero, compare the different details and main points that each student has included. Students complete questions 5 and 6.

Go through the guidance on inverted commas. Take students through the example and point out conventions such as identifying who is speaking, use of 'said', opening speech marks, ending with a full stop and then closing speech marks. In pairs, students to work through questions 1 and 2 of **Activity 6**.

Plenary

Ask students to show their peers how they have punctuated the sentences in question 2, Activity 6 to include the quotations.

Homework

Complete question 3 of Activity 6.

Answers

Activity 2
2 a Main point: The team has many talented players. Main image: Background showing the Man Utd football team.
   b Details: the players include Rio Ferdinand, Ryan Giggs and Dimitar Berbatov. Berbatov joined the club on 1st September 2008 and he was also captain of the Bulgarian national team from 2006 to 2010.

Activity 3
2 a Wayne Rooney is famous all over the world.
   b Because he's a top striker for Manchester United and England.
3 Rooney scored a hat-trick and has since gone on to score many goals for his club.
4 He has been selected on many occasions to to play for England, playing in the 2006 and 2010 World Cups. He was named the PFA Players' Player of the Year in April 2010.

Writing lesson plans

Student book pages 90–93

8 Writing effective sentences

Aim
- Use correct grammar, including correct and consistent use of tense.

Lesson learning and objectives
- Write in complete and clear sentences. Write in different types of sentences and punctuate sentences correctly.

Lesson starter: individual/pair work

Discuss the importance of writing clear sentences, using different types of sentences and correct punctuation. Draw students' attention to the Watch out! box on page 90 and remind them of earlier work on punctuation and use of connectives. Take them through the simple sentences checklist and discuss the use of a verb. Remind students that this is useful as a checklist for their writing and a helpful revision tool. In pairs, students work through questions 1, 2 and 3 of **Activity 1**. Feed back through whole-class discussion.

Main teaching and learning

Individually, students complete questions 1 and 2 of **Activity 2**, then swap with a partner and compare. Take students through the guidance on linking simple sentences and discuss the examples.

In pairs, students work through **Activity 3**. Share ideas with another pair and discuss how well their longer sentences worked and how well connectives were used. Take feedback in class discussion. Read the guidance on varying your sentences and refer students to the Top tip box on page 92. Remind them that the full stop, question mark and exclamation mark all act as full stops to end sentences.

Individually, students complete question 1 of **Activity 4**, then complete question 2 in pairs. Students then complete **Activity 5** individually. If possible, provide examples of a blog to ensure that students understand the form. Direct them to use the bullets as a checklist and share their blogs with a partner when finished.

Read the punctuating sentences guidance with students. Emphasise that this is good for reference and revision, and use the Top tip box on page 93 to reinforce messages about sentence construction.

If possible, enlarge Text C and make copies for paired students to work through for questions 1 and 2 of **Activity 6**. They could use highlighters to show where one sentence ends and another begins. Share their ideas with the class, discussing the correctly punctuated form. If some students have different versions, use the opportunity to discuss reasons for choices. Ensure there is agreement and understanding at the end of the discussion. Encourage students to make changes if necessary and display correct versions to reinforce learning. In pairs, students work through **Activity 7**.

Plenary

Share some of the responses to Text D, discuss feedback exchanged in pairs and reiterate the key learning points from the lesson.

Homework

Ask students to write their own paragraph about a hobby or interest, using what has been learned in this lesson as well as previous writing lessons.

Answers

The activities in this lesson are open student writing tasks, for which answers have not been provided.

Student book pages 94–97

9 Practising writing clearly and logically (1)

Aim
- Write clearly and coherently, including an appropriate level of detail.
- Present information in a logical sequence.

Lesson learning and objectives
- Practise writing a complete text. Organise points logically and improve spelling.

Lesson starter: individual/pair work

Explain the importance of being able to write a complete text that is organised logically with accurate spelling. Remind them that accuracy of spelling, grammar and punctuation are features of successful writing.

Read Task A of **Activity 1** with students. In pairs, ask them to establish audience, purpose and style. Feed back in class discussion.

Main teaching and learning

Read the section on gathering your ideas with students and direct them in pairs to write a set of instructions using the guidance. Make sure they do not write about making a sandwich, as that follows in Activity 3. In feedback discuss with students how this is relevant to real-life situations, e.g. when we need to write or give instructions and when we need to follow them.

In pairs, students complete **Activity 2**. Give feedback through whole-class discussion. Remind students what is meant by form, and refer to page 95 if necessary. There is also an opportunity to revisit use of connectives. Students should read the Top tip box on page 94 as they undertake question 3.

Students work through **Activity 3**, independently or in pairs as directed. In class discussion, ask students what they needed to change to ensure their instructions were clear.

Students go back to the same pairs they were in for Activity 2 to work through and complete **Activity 4**. During class feedback, compare instructions using numbered lists and time connectives, and comment on the effectiveness of each approach.

Read through the guidance on using the right words, including the Watch out! box on page 96 with students. In pairs, students work through **Activity 5**.

Individually, students work through **Activity 6**, then swap with a partner to discuss ways to improve. Take students through the guidance on improving your spelling.

In pairs, students work through **Activity 7**. It would be useful to supply dictionaries. Remind them of *there, their, they're* as examples of words that sound the same, but that have different spellings and meanings. Students complete **Activity 8** in pairs.

Plenary

Invite students to advise on correct spellings for Ivan's draft in Activity 8. Check that students are clear on spelling strategies, giving/following instructions, using correct names, and using connectives.

Answers

Activities 1 to 7 are open student writing tasks, for which answers have not been provided.

Activity 8
2 Incorrect spellings: Wednsday, diffcult, you're, too, garaje, their, wen, your, its.

Writing lesson plans

Student book pages 98–101

10 Practising writing clearly and logically (2)

Aim
- Use language, format and structure suitable for purpose and audience.
- Use correct grammar, including correct and consistent use of tense.
- Ensure written work includes generally accurate punctuation and spelling and that meaning is clear.

Lesson learning and objectives
- Practise writing a complete text in the form of briefing notes. Organise points logically and use correct verb tenses.

Lesson starter: individual/pair work

Explain that this lesson will lead to writing briefing notes and students will be able to apply what they have learned to the writing process. Go through the guidance on page 98 of the student book and draw attention to the Top tip box advice.

Read Text A of **Activity 1** with students. Discuss with students how briefing notes are used in real-life situations. Reproduce the table separately so that students can complete Activity 1 in pairs. Feed back in class discussion.

Main teaching and learning

Remind students how tables are used to record information and link back to Reading Lesson 11. In pairs, ask students to discuss the features that make the text easy to follow.

Read Task A of **Activity 2** with students. Discuss question 2a as a class and direct students to make notes on audience, purpose and form. Discuss the headings in question 3. Explain that this is the structure for their briefing notes and will provide the basis of their writing plan.

In pairs, students work through question 4, then complete questions 5 and 6 individually. Refer students back to the example of Text A as well as the bullet points listed in question 6 of Activity 2.

For question 7, get students to swap drafts with a partner, check each other's work and feed back in class discussion.

Discuss the verb tenses guidance and the Top tip box on page 101. Go through the three main verb tenses, when each one is used, and the example provided. In pairs, students complete questions 1 and 2 of **Activity 3**. Individually, students complete questions 3a and b, before swapping briefing notes with a partner and reviewing each other's work, checking generally and also looking at verb tenses.

Plenary

Discuss as a class key things learned and any areas that need clarifying, including verbs.

Homework

Individually, write up the draft briefing notes into a final version.

Answers

Activity 1
2 b Introduction: A. Background: C. Considerations: B. At the concert: D.
  c Bullet points, short sentences, sensible and logical order of information.

Activity 2
2 a Audience: local MP. Purpose: for the MP to find out some information about education. Form: briefing notes.

Activity 3
2 Are, were, follow, will get.

How students will be assessed – Reading

Students' reading is assessed in one 45-minute exam. The total number of marks for the Reading paper is 20.

The Reading paper is divided into two sections: A and B. Each section has a text to read and questions to answer about it. Each question states the number of marks it is worth. The two texts are on the same subject or theme. Students will be given space to write their answers.

The table below shows the types of questions students will be asked and what they should do in each case.

Types of question	What students should do
Multiple choice.	Select the correct option to complete an unfinished sentence or to answer a question. Put a cross in a box to show their answer.
Find a number of pieces of information and evidence in the text.	Give short written answers.
Identify features of the text that tell you what kind of text it is.	Give a short written answer **or** select several options from a list, putting a cross in a box to show their answer.
Respond to the text by using information in it.	Write a short answer based on information from the text. There will be a number of possible answers.

Assessment

How students will be assessed – Speaking, listening and communication

You will assess your students' speaking, listening and communication skills. They may take time ahead of their assessments to research and prepare what they want to say and they can use notes to help them on the day.

The table below shows the tasks students will have to complete and what they should do in each case. The two discussions must have different contexts and subjects, including some unfamiliar subjects.

Type of task	Who with?	Time	Students must show that they can
Formal discussion	About four others	About 15 minutes	Make relevant and extended contributions to discussions. Allow for and respond to others' input. Prepare for and contribute to discussions of ideas and opinions.
Informal discussion	Up to four others	About 15 minutes	Make different kinds of contributions. Pesent information and points of view clearly. Use appropriate language.

How students will be assessed – Writing

Students' writing is assessed in one 45-minute exam. There are two tasks which assess their writing skills. The total number of marks for the Writing paper is 25: 15 marks for Task 1 and 10 marks for Task 2.

For each task, students will be given some information. They will then be given a writing task based on it. They will be told what form to write in and given some guidance on what to include.

The table below shows what students will be assessed on and what they must show they can do.

What students will be assessed on	Students must show that they can
Form, communication and purpose	Use the correct format for their writing, for example, a correctly laid-out letter.
	Organise their writing logically.
	Communicate effectively the information that the reader needs.
	Use appropriate language for the purpose.
	Write to meet the purpose; for example, to inform.
Spelling, punctuation and grammar	Ensure their spelling and grammar are generally accurate and the reader can understand their meaning.
	Use a range of punctuation generally correctly.

Reading

Write your name here

Surname _____ Other names _____

Edexcel Functional Skills

Centre Number ☐☐☐☐☐ Candidate Number ☐☐☐☐

English

Level 1
Component 2: Reading

sample assessment material
Time: 45 minutes

Paper Reference(s)
E102/01

You may use a dictionary.
You do not need to write in complete sentences.

Total Marks

Instructions

- Use **black** ink or ball-point pen.
- **Fill in the boxes** at the top of this page with your name, centre number and candidate number.
- Answer **all** questions.
- Answer the questions in the spaces provided – *there may be more space than you need.*
- Dictionaries may be used.

Information

- The total mark for this paper is 20.
- The marks for **each** question are shown in brackets – *use this as a guide as to how much time to spend on each question.*

Advice

- Read each question carefully before you start to answer it.
- Keep an eye on the time.
- Try to answer every question.
- Check your answers if you have time at the end.

Turn over ▶

SECTION A

Read Text A and answer questions 1 – 6.

Text A

You are interested in fun ways of getting fit. You look at the internet to see what sort of activities might be interesting. You have found this web page.

Welcome to The Silly Army website

The Silly Army is a new alternative outdoor sports club, based in Bournemouth, Dorset.

We invented The Silly Army as an excuse for adults of all ages to run around like kids, playing silly games and sports like we used to do at school. Some of our favourite games include tag bulldog, dodgeball, spacehopper polo and spacehopper rugby, ultimate frisbee and five-a-side tennis. We also play some woodland-based games and beach games, when the weather is right, and organise activity trips for members when possible.

Our regular meeting place is 1pm every Sunday at King's Park between the football pitches and the children's play area, just behind the cricket pavilion.

There is no charge and anyone over the age of 18 is welcome to come and join in. You don't have to be super fit or good at sports: enthusiasm, ideas, a bit of imagination and the ability to play games that involve running around for fun are what count!

GO AHEAD – BE SILLY AND CONTACT US!

Menu: HOME, NEWS, CONTACT US, PHOTO GALLERY 1, PHOTO GALLERY 2, WHERE TO FIND US, SILLY MEMBER PROFILE, EVENTS CALENDER, ABOUT US

Adapted from www.spanglefish.com/sillyarmy/©The Silly Army

Answer questions 1 to 3 with a cross in the box ☒. If you change your mind about an answer, put a line through the box ☒ and then mark your new answer with a cross ☒.

1   The **main** purpose of this web page is to:

A	☐	describe the playground games that children play at school
B	☐	invite web page readers to join in the activities at the club
C	☐	persuade web page readers that silly games are better than usual sports
D	☐	inform web page readers about the activity trips that are on offer

(Total for Question 1 = 1 mark)

2   The Silly Army was invented to provide:

A	☐	more sports clubs for the area
B	☐	somewhere for adults to meet
C	☐	woodland sports for people
D	☐	somewhere for adults to play silly games

(Total for Question 2 = 1 mark)

3   Which of these statements about The Silly Army is true?

A	☐	It is for under-18s.
B	☐	It is free of charge.
C	☐	It meets monthly.
D	☐	It meets on weekdays.

(Total for Question 3 = 1 mark)

4 Name **one** sport/game offered by The Silly Army.

....

(Total for Question 4 = 1 mark)

5 List **two** features of Text A that show it is a web page.

You do **not** need to write in sentences.

1 ....

2 ....

(Total for Question 5 = 2 marks)

6 Find **two** important pieces of information from Text A that you would need if you wanted to visit the club.

You do **not** need to write in sentences.

1 ....

....

2 ....

....

(Total for Question 6 = 2 marks)

7 What type of person would like to join The Silly Army?

Give **two** suggestions using the information from Text A.

You do **not** need to write in sentences.

1 ....

....

2 ....

....

(Total for Question 7 = 2 marks)

TOTAL FOR SECTION A = 10 MARKS

SECTION B

Read Text B and answer questions 8 – 13.

Text B

You have joined The Silly Army and have been sent this letter before you attend your first session.

102 The Broadway
Bournemouth
Dorset
BH1 4DA

10th June 2010

Dear New Recruit

Health and Safety Guidance for New Members

Thank you for your interest in The Silly Army. Health and safety is important to us to ensure that we can be silly, but safe when getting fit. Please take a few moments to read through the following guidance before you attend your first session.

All our helpers are trained in first aid, and there are radio links in place between all the helpers. A thorough risk assessment has been undertaken for all the activities we run to make sure our members stay safe and have fun.

Things you will need:
- Outdoor and wet-weather clothing that you don't mind getting dirty
- Shoes with good non-slip soles
- Sense of fun!

We provide all sport equipment, including helmets and protective padding for the games.

If you are not used to playing sport, you should make sure that your doctor says that you are fit to participate. If you need any additional support, or have any medical conditions such as asthma, you must let the helper organising your game know BEFORE you start playing.

Keeping our members injury free is important, so make sure you are fully warmed up before the activities and that you cool down appropriately after the fun activities like spacehopper polo.

We look forward to welcoming you at the club soon. If you have any questions please feel free to contact me directly on 07771234568.

Yours sincerely

Sam Elkins

The Silly Army Leader

Logo ©The Silly Army

Answer question 8 with a cross in the box ☒ you think is correct. If you change your mind about an answer, put a line through the box ☒ and then mark your new answer with a cross ☒.

8 What is the **main** purpose of this letter?

A	☐	To persuade you to join the club.
B	☐	To make you visit your doctor.
C	☐	To inform you of the activities at the club.
D	☐	To give you advice before your first visit.

(Total for Question 8 = 1 mark)

Answer question 9 with a cross in the two boxes ☒ you think are correct. If you change your mind about an answer, put a line through the box ☒ and then mark your new answer with a cross ☒.

9 Identify **two** features from the list below that show that Text B is a letter.

A	☐	bullet points
B	☐	use of Yours sincerely
C	☐	heading
D	☐	address and date
E	☐	contact number
F	☐	logo

(Total for Question 9 = 2 marks)

10 Identify **two** things you are told in Text B you must do **before** you take part in activities with The Silly Army?

You do **not** need to write in sentences.

1 ....

....

2 ....

....

(Total for Question 10 = 2 marks)

11 Your friend wants to come to The Silly Army with you, but is a little worried about health and safety.

Using Text B give **two** reasons to reassure your friend that The Silly Army takes health and safety seriously.

You do **not** need to write in sentences.

1 ....

....

2 ....

....

(Total for Question 11 = 2 marks)

12 According to Text B, how should you contact The Silly Army if you have a question?

You do **not** need to write in sentences.

....

(Total for Question 12 = 1 mark)

13 You want some friends to come along to The Silly Army, so you send a group email.

Using the information from Text B, what **two** points about The Silly Army would you include in your email?

You do **not** need to write in sentences.

1 ....

....

2 ....

....

(Total for Question 13 = 2 marks)

TOTAL FOR SECTION B = 10 MARKS
TOTAL FOR PAPER = 20 MARKS

Mark scheme: Reading

Section A

Question Number	Answer	Mark
1	B – invite web page readers to join in the activities at the club	(1)

Question Number	Answer	Mark
2	D – somewhere for adults to play silly games	(1)

Question Number	Answer	Mark
3	B – It is free of charge.	(1)

Question Number	Answer	Mark
4	Answers may include: • tag bulldog (1) • dodgeball (1) • spacehopper polo (1) • spacehopper rugby (1) • ultimate frisbee (1) • five-a-side tennis (1)	(1)

Question Number	Answer	Mark
5	Answers may include: • menu (1) • web page address (1) • search box (1) • can click on links, e.g. map, advertisements (1) • scroll bar (1) Accept any reasonable answer, based on the text, up to a maximum of **two** marks.	(2)

Question Number	Answer	Mark
6	Answers may include: • time 1pm (1) • Sunday (1) • King's Park (behind cricket pavilion)(1) • email them/contact them (1) • based in Bournemouth (1) Accept any reasonable answer, based on the text, up to a maximum of **two** marks.	(2)

Question Number	Answer	Mark
7	Answers may include: • enthusiastic (1) • have good ideas (1) • imaginative (1) • have a sense of fun (1) • able to run around (1) • not very fit (1) • not very good at sports (1) Accept any reasonable answer, based on the text, up to a maximum of **two** marks.	(2)

Assessment

Section B

Question Number	Answer	Mark
8	D – To give you advice before your first visit.	(1)

Question Number	Answer	Mark
9	B – use of Yours sincerely D – address and date One mark for each correct answer.	(2)

Question Number	Answer	Mark
10	• Bring suitable outdoor and wet weather clothes (1) • Bring non-slip footwear (1) • See your doctor if you need to (1) • Let helper know of any medical conditions (1) • Make sure you are fully warmed up (1) One mark for each correct answer, up to a maximum of **two** marks.	(2)

Question Number	Answer	Mark
11	Answers may include: • they tell you health and safety is important to them (1) • helpers are trained in first aid (1) • they provide helmets (1) • they provide protective padding (1) • they give you a number for other questions (1) • they have carried out a risk assessment for all activities (1) Accept any reasonable answer, based on the text, up to a maximum of **two** marks.	(2)

Question Number	Answer	Mark
12	Accept • telephone (Sam Elkin)(on 07771234568) (1) One mark for a correct answer. Do **not** accept an answer from outside the text, e.g. email.	(1)

Question Number	Answer	Mark
13	Answers may include: • it's local (Bournemouth) (1) • fun activities, e.g. spacehopper polo (1) • can get fit (1) • make it safe for members (1) Accept any reasonable answer, based on the text, up to a maximum of **two** marks.	(2)

Writing

Assessment

Write your name here

Surname | Other names

Edexcel
Functional Skills

English

Level 1
Component 3: Writing

sample assessment material
Time: 45 minutes

Paper Reference(s)
E103/01

You may use a dictionary.

Total Marks

Instructions

- Use **black** ink or ball-point pen.
- **Fill in the boxes** at the top of this page with your name, centre number and candidate number.
- Answer **both** tasks.
- Answer the tasks in the spaces provided – *there may be more space than you need*.
- Dictionaries may be used.

Information

- The total mark for this paper is 25.
- The marks for **each** task are shown in brackets – *use this as a guide as to how much time to spend on each task*.
- You will be assessed on spelling, punctuation and grammar in both tasks.

Advice

- Read each task carefully before you start to answer it.
- Keep an eye on the time.
- Try to complete both tasks.
- Check your answers if you have time at the end.

Turn over ▶

Assessment

There are **two** tasks which assess your writing skills.

Remember that spelling, punctuation and grammar will be assessed in **both** tasks.

Task 1

Information

You are a member of a group trying to raise money for your local hospital. You receive the email below from one of your group.

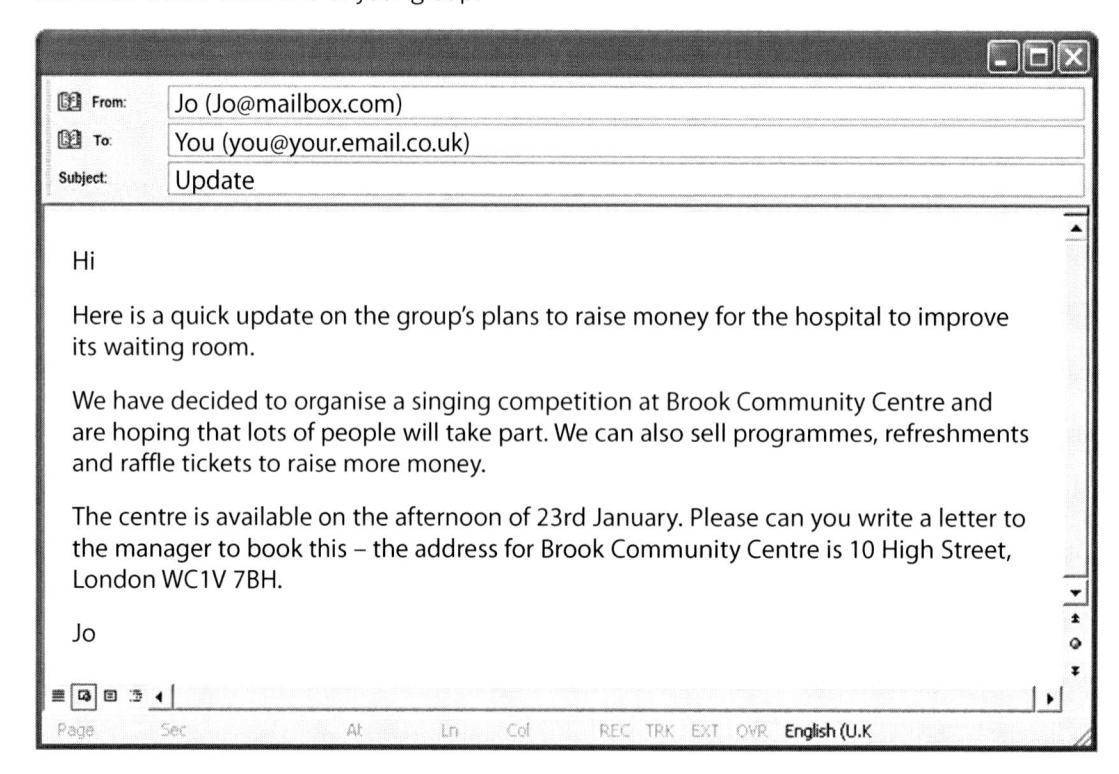

From: Jo (Jo@mailbox.com)
To: You (you@your.email.co.uk)
Subject: Update

Hi

Here is a quick update on the group's plans to raise money for the hospital to improve its waiting room.

We have decided to organise a singing competition at Brook Community Centre and are hoping that lots of people will take part. We can also sell programmes, refreshments and raffle tickets to raise more money.

The centre is available on the afternoon of 23rd January. Please can you write a letter to the manager to book this – the address for Brook Community Centre is 10 High Street, London WC1V 7BH.

Jo

Writing Task

Write a letter to Jill Smith, the manager of Brook Community Centre, to book the centre for the singing competition.

In your letter you should:

- introduce yourself and the reason for raising money
- ask to book the centre
- explain how you want to use the centre.

Remember to set your letter out correctly.

(15)

Begin your letter on the next page.

(TOTAL FOR TASK 1 = 15 MARKS)

Task 2

Information

You recently used the website below to buy a pair of these trainers.

ShoeWorld.co.uk

High Top Fashion Trainers

£36.99

★★★★★

(23 customer reviews)

Write a Review

Colour: **Black**

Code: **111777777**

Product information

Black High Top Trainers. Canvas upper with white laces and white rubber sole and toe, man-made inner.

Writing Task

You have only worn your trainers a few times and they are now falling apart.

Write an email to the company to complain.

You may wish to include:

- how long you have had the trainers
- what the fault is
- what you want them to do about it.

(10)

Begin your answer on the next page.

Assessment

New Message

From: you@your.email.co.uk
To: CustomerServices@ShoeWorld.co.uk
Subject: Complaint

(TOTAL FOR TASK 2 = 10 MARKS)

TOTAL FOR PAPER = 25 MARKS

Assessment

Mark scheme: Writing

Task	
1	Write a letter to Jill Smith, the manager of Brook Community Centre, to book the centre for the singing competition. In your letter you should: • introduce yourself and the reason for raising money • ask to book the centre • explain how you want to use the centre. Remember to set your letter out correctly. (15 marks)
	Indicative content
	• Response set out with attention to letter layout. • Uses paragraphing and other organisational features. • Attempts to use appropriate tone/language when explaining the singing competition to the manager. • Opens and closes the letter clearly.

Mark	A: Form, communication and purpose
0	No rewardable material.
1–3	• Communicates relevant information and ideas at a basic level. • Information is presented with limited sequencing of ideas. • Uses language, format and structure for specific audience and purpose to a limited extent. • Limited use of appropriate layout of a letter (address, date, open and close conventions).
4–6	• Communicates relevant information and ideas with some success. • Information is presented with some logical sequencing of ideas, although this is not sustained throughout the response. • Uses language, format and structure for specific audience and purpose, for some of the response. • Some use of appropriate layout of a letter (address, date, open and close conventions), though there may be omissions or inconsistencies.
7–9	• Communicates relevant information and ideas successfully, although there may be minor lapses. • Information is presented with a logical sequencing of ideas and this is evident for the majority of the response. • Uses language, format and structure for specific audience and purpose throughout the response, although there may be occasional slips/omissions. • Appropriate use of layout of a letter (address, date, open and close conventions), any omissions do not detract from the overall quality of the response.

Mark	B: Spelling, punctuation and grammar
0	No rewardable material.
1–2	• There is limited use of correct grammar and use of tense is minimal. • Spelling and punctuation are used with limited accuracy and errors will often affect clarity of meaning.
3–4	• There is some correct use of grammar and some correct use of tense although not sustained throughout the response. • Spelling and punctuation are used with some accuracy although errors will sometimes affect clarity of meaning.
5–6	• There is correct use of grammar and consistent use of tense throughout the response, although there may be occasional errors. • Spelling and punctuation are used with general accuracy and meaning is clearly conveyed, with only occasional lapses.

Assessment

Task	
2	You have only worn your trainers a few times and now they are falling apart. Write an email to the company to complain. You may wish to include: - how long you have had the trainers - what the fault is - what you want them to do about it. (10 marks)
	Indicative content
	- Uses relevant organisational features. - Uses appropriate tone/language when writing about the trainers. - Show awareness of audience such as using features of email response.

Mark	A: Form, communication and purpose
0	No rewardable material.
1–2	- Communicates relevant information and ideas at a basic level. - Information is presented with limited sequencing of ideas. - Uses language, format and structure for specific audience and purpose to a limited extent. - Response has limited level of appropriate detail.
3–4	- Communicates relevant information and ideas with some success. - Information is presented with some logical sequencing of ideas, although this is not sustained throughout the response. - Uses language, format and structure for specific audience and purpose, for some of the response. - Response has some level of appropriate detail.
5–6	- Communicates relevant information and ideas successfully, although there may be minor lapses. - Information is presented with a logical sequencing of ideas and this is evident for the majority of the response. - Uses language, format and structure for specific audience and purpose throughout the response, although there may be occasional slips/omissions. - Response has developed level of appropriate detail.

Mark	B: Spelling, punctuation and grammar
0	No rewardable material.
1–2	- There is some use of correct grammar and some appropriate use of tense. - Spelling and punctuation are used with limited accuracy and errors will sometimes affect clarity of meaning.
3–4	- There is mostly correct use of grammar and mostly consistent use of tense throughout the response, although there may be occasional errors. - Spelling and punctuation are used mostly with accuracy, with some lapses.

Sample Reading answers – pass

Reading Level 1 pass answer

SECTION A

Read Text A and answer questions 1 – 6.

Text A

You are interested in fun ways of getting fit. You look at the internet to see what sort of activities might be interesting. You have found this web page.

Welcome to The Silly Army website

The Silly Army is a new alternative outdoor sports club, based in Bournemouth, Dorset.

We invented The Silly Army as an excuse for adults of all ages to run around like kids, playing silly games and sports like we used to do at school. Some of our favourite games include tag bulldog, dodgeball, spacehopper polo and spacehopper rugby, ultimate frisbee and five-a-side tennis. We also play some woodland-based games and beach games, when the weather is right, and organise activity trips for members when possible.

Our regular meeting place is 1pm every Sunday at King's Park between the football pitches and the children's play area, just behind the cricket pavilion.

There is no charge and anyone over the age of 18 is welcome to come and join in. You don't have to be super fit or good at sports:

enthusiasm, ideas, a bit of imagination and the ability to play games that involve running around for fun are what count!

GO AHEAD – BE SILLY AND CONTACT US!

Adapted from www.spanglefish.com/sillyarmy/©The Silly Army

Assessment

Answer questions 1 to 3 with a cross in the box ☒. If you change your mind about an answer, put a line through the box ▨ and then mark your new answer with a cross ☒.

1 The **main** purpose of this web page is to:

A	☐	describe the playground games that children play at school
B	☒	invite web page readers to join in the activities at the club
C	☐	persuade web page readers that silly games are better than usual sports
D	☐	inform web page readers about the activity trips that are on offer

This is correct because the text describes the activities on offer and states that everyone is 'welcome to come and join in'. 1 mark.

(Total for Question 1 = 1 mark)

2 The Silly Army was invented to provide:

A	☐	more sports clubs for the area
B	☐	somewhere for adults to meet
C	☐	woodland sports for people
D	☒	somewhere for adults to play silly games

This is correct because in the second paragraph it says 'We invented the Silly Army as an excuse for adults of all ages to run around like kids, playing silly games…' 1 mark.

(Total for Question 2 = 1 mark)

3 Which of these statements about The Silly Army is true?

A	☐	It is for under-18s.
B	☒	It is free of charge.
C	☐	It meets monthly.
D	☐	It meets on weekdays.

This is correct because in the final paragraph it states 'There is no charge.' 1 mark.

(Total for Question 3 = 1 mark)

4 Name **one** sport/game offered by The Silly Army.

Tag bulldog

This is correct because tag bulldog is listed as 'one of our favourite games'.

(Total for Question 4 = 1 mark)

© Pearson Education Limited 2010 75

Assessment

5 List **two** features of Text A that show it is a web page.

You do **not** need to write in sentences.

1. Address bar
2. it says click for map

> These answers are correct because they are both features showing this is a web page. They could be improved to make sure the examiner gives the mark by i) giving the actual address of the web page and ii) explaining that this means you are expected to click on a link to get more information. 2 marks.

(Total for Question 5 = 2 marks)

6 Find **two** important pieces of information from Text A that you would need if you wanted to visit the club.

You do **not** need to write in sentences.

1. it's on Sundays every week
2. they meet in King's Park

> This is correct because these pieces of information tell you where and when Silly Army meetings take place. 2 marks.

(Total for Question 6 = 2 marks)

7 What type of person would like to join The Silly Army?

Give **two** suggestions using the information from Text A.

You do **not** need to write in sentences.

1. people who would like to have fun
2. people with a bit of imagination

> Both of these are mentioned in the final sentence which describes the qualities you need for the Silly Army. 2 marks.

(Total for Question 7 = 2 marks)

TOTAL FOR SECTION A = 10 MARKS

SECTION B

Read Text B and answer questions 8 – 13.

Text B

You have joined The Silly Army and have been sent this letter before you attend your first session.

102 The Broadway
Bournemouth
Dorset
BH1 4DA

10th June 2010

Dear New Recruit

Health and Safety Guidance for New Members

Thank you for your interest in The Silly Army. Health and safety is important to us to ensure that we can be silly, but safe when getting fit. Please take a few moments to read through the following guidance before you attend your first session.

All our helpers are trained in first aid, and there are radio links in place between all the helpers. A thorough risk assessment has been undertaken for all the activities we run to make sure our members stay safe and have fun.

Things you will need:
- Outdoor and wet-weather clothing that you don't mind getting dirty
- Shoes with good non-slip soles
- Sense of fun!

We provide all sport equipment, including helmets and protective padding for the games.

If you are not used to playing sport, you should make sure that your doctor says that you are fit to participate. If you need any additional support, or have any medical conditions such as asthma, you must let the helper organising your game know BEFORE you start playing.

Keeping our members injury free is important, so make sure you are fully warmed up before the activities and that you cool down appropriately after the fun activities like spacehopper polo.

We look forward to welcoming you at the club soon. If you have any questions please feel free to contact me directly on 07771234568.

Yours sincerely

Sam Elkins

The Silly Army Leader

Logo ©The Silly Army

Assessment

Answer question 8 with a cross in the box ☒ you think is correct. If you change your mind about an answer, put a line through the box ☒ and then mark your new answer with a cross ☒.

8 What is the **main** purpose of this letter?

A	☐	To persuade you to join the club.
B	☐	To make you visit your doctor.
C	☐	To inform you of the activities at the club.
D	☒	To give you advice before your first visit.

This is correct because the letter asks you to 'read through the following guidance before you attend your first session'. 1 mark.

(Total for Question 8 = 1 mark)

Answer question 9 with a cross in the two boxes ☒ you think are correct. If you change your mind about an answer, put a line through the box ☒ and then mark your new answer with a cross ☒.

9 Identify **two** features from the list below that show that Text B is a letter.

A	☐	bullet points
B	☒	use of Yours sincerely
C	☐	heading
D	☒	address and date
E	☐	contact number
F	☐	logo

(Total for Question 9 = 2 marks)

Both of these are features that show Text B is a letter. 2 marks.

10 Identify **two** things you are told in Text B you must do **before** you take part in activities with The Silly Army?

You do **not** need to write in sentences.

1 tell them about any illness that you have

2 warm up appropriately

These pieces of information are both part of the guidance given to new recruits in Text B. 2 marks.

(Total for Question 10 = 2 marks)

Assessment

11 Your friend wants to come to The Silly Army with you, but is a little worried about health and safety.

Using Text B give **two** reasons to reassure your friend that The Silly Army takes health and safety seriously.

You do **not** need to write in sentences.

1 they provide free safety equipment for people — *These pieces of information are both stated in Text B. 2 marks.*

2 helpers are trained in first aid

(Total for Question 11 = 2 marks)

12 According to Text B, how should you contact The Silly Army if you have a question?

You do **not** need to write in sentences.

Contact the Silly Army leader directly on 07771234568

(Total for Question 12 = 1 mark)

This is correct because this telephone number is given in the final paragraph of the letter. 1 mark.

13 You want some friends to come along to The Silly Army, so you send a group email.

Using the information from Text B, what **two** points about The Silly Army would you include in your email?

You do **not** need to write in sentences.

1 fun activities like spacehopper polo — *Both these points are described in Text B and might persuade someone to join in. 2 marks.*

2 they will look after your health and safety

(Total for Question 13 = 2 marks)

TOTAL FOR SECTION B = 10 MARKS
TOTAL FOR PAPER = 20 MARKS

Sample Reading answers – fail

Reading Level 1 fail answer

SECTION A

Read Text A and answer questions 1 – 6.

Text A

You are interested in fun ways of getting fit. You look at the internet to see what sort of activities might be interesting. You have found this web page.

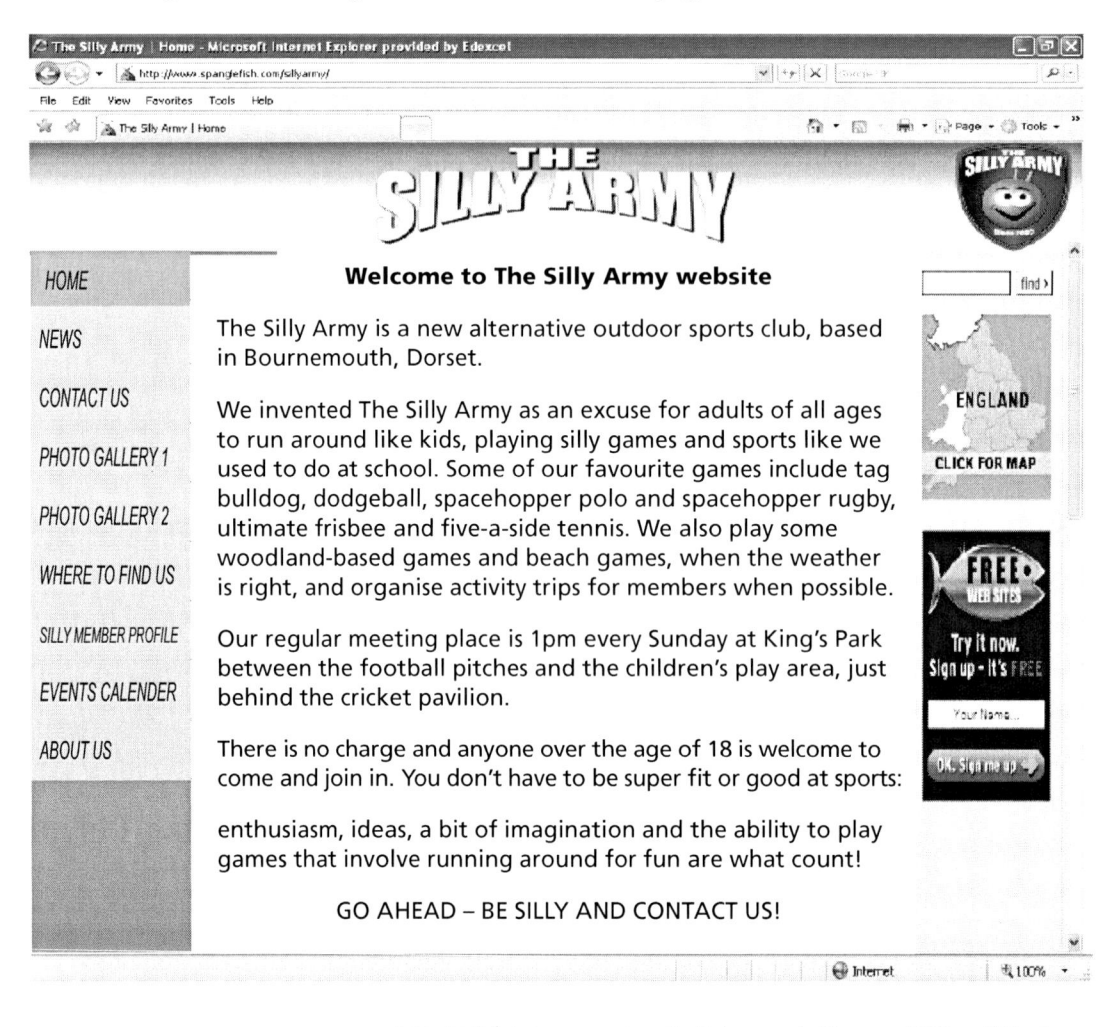

Welcome to The Silly Army website

The Silly Army is a new alternative outdoor sports club, based in Bournemouth, Dorset.

We invented The Silly Army as an excuse for adults of all ages to run around like kids, playing silly games and sports like we used to do at school. Some of our favourite games include tag bulldog, dodgeball, spacehopper polo and spacehopper rugby, ultimate frisbee and five-a-side tennis. We also play some woodland-based games and beach games, when the weather is right, and organise activity trips for members when possible.

Our regular meeting place is 1pm every Sunday at King's Park between the football pitches and the children's play area, just behind the cricket pavilion.

There is no charge and anyone over the age of 18 is welcome to come and join in. You don't have to be super fit or good at sports: enthusiasm, ideas, a bit of imagination and the ability to play games that involve running around for fun are what count!

GO AHEAD – BE SILLY AND CONTACT US!

Adapted from www.spanglefish.com/sillyarmy/©The Silly Army

Assessment

Answer questions 1 to 3 with a cross in the box ☒. If you change your mind about an answer, put a line through the box ☒ and then mark your new answer with a cross ☒.

1 The **main** purpose of this web page is to:

A	☒	describe the playground games that children play at school
B	☐	invite web page readers to join in the activities at the club
C	☒	persuade web page readers that silly games are better than usual sports
D	☒	inform web page readers about the activity trips that are on offer

> This is incorrect because Text A is describing games played by the Silly Army.

> This is incorrect because the text does not compare these games with other sports.

> This is incorrect because the trips are not described and are only a small part of what goes on at the Silly Army.

(Total for Question 1 = 1 mark)

2 The Silly Army was invented to provide:

A	☒	more sports clubs for the area
B	☒	somewhere for adults to meet
C	☒	woodland sports for people
D	☐	somewhere for adults to play silly games

> This is incorrect because this is not a reason given in Text A.

> This is incorrect because the Silly Army is not for all adults, just for those who wish to play 'silly games'.

> This is incorrect because 'woodland-based games' are only a small part of what goes on.

(Total for Question 2 = 1 mark)

3 Which of these statements about The Silly Army is true?

A	☒	It is for under-18s.
B	☐	It is free of charge.
C	☒	It meets monthly.
D	☒	It meets on weekdays.

> This is incorrect because you have to be over 18.

> Both of these are incorrect because the Silly Army meets every Sunday.

(Total for Question 3 = 1 mark)

© Pearson Education Limited 2010

Assessment

4 Name **one** sport/game offered by The Silly Army.

Spacehopper

> This is incorrect because although spacehoppers are used, this is not the name of a sport or game. Correct answers would have been 'spacehopper polo' or 'spacehopper rugby'.

(Total for Question 4 = 1 mark)

5 List **two** features of Text A that show it is a web page.

You do **not** need to write in sentences.

1 information

2 the logos

> Neither of these answers is correct because both may be a feature of any kind of text or document.

(Total for Question 5 = 2 marks)

6 Find **two** important pieces of information from Text A that you would need if you wanted to visit the club.

You do **not** need to write in sentences.

1 People are interested in getting fit

2 what time to get there

> Answer 1 is incorrect because it is not information given in Text A. Answer 2 gives the type of information you would need rather than the actual information itself – i.e. the Silly Army meets at 1 p.m.

(Total for Question 6 = 2 marks)

7 What type of person would like to join The Silly Army?

Give **two** suggestions using the information from Text A.

You do **not** need to write in sentences.

1 they have to be fit

2 people who have spare time

> 1 is incorrect because Text A says 'you don't have to be super-fit'. Answer 2 may be true but does not get a mark because it does not use information from Text A.

(Total for Question 7 = 2 marks)

TOTAL FOR SECTION A = 10 MARKS

SECTION B

Read Text B and answer questions 8 – 13.

Text B

You have joined The Silly Army and have been sent this letter before you attend your first session.

---

102 The Broadway
Bournemouth
Dorset
BH1 4DA

10th June 2010

Dear New Recruit

Health and Safety Guidance for New Members

Thank you for your interest in The Silly Army. Health and safety is important to us to ensure that we can be silly, but safe when getting fit. Please take a few moments to read through the following guidance before you attend your first session.

All our helpers are trained in first aid, and there are radio links in place between all the helpers. A thorough risk assessment has been undertaken for all the activities we run to make sure our members stay safe and have fun.

Things you will need:
- Outdoor and wet-weather clothing that you don't mind getting dirty
- Shoes with good non-slip soles
- Sense of fun!

We provide all sport equipment, including helmets and protective padding for the games.

If you are not used to playing sport, you should make sure that your doctor says that you are fit to participate. If you need any additional support, or have any medical conditions such as asthma, you must let the helper organising your game know BEFORE you start playing.

Keeping our members injury free is important, so make sure you are fully warmed up before the activities and that you cool down appropriately after the fun activities like spacehopper polo.

We look forward to welcoming you at the club soon. If you have any questions please feel free to contact me directly on 07771234568.

Yours sincerely

Sam Elkins

The Silly Army Leader

Logo ©The Silly Army

Assessment

Answer question 8 with a cross in the box ☒ you think is correct. If you change your mind about an answer, put a line through the box ☒ and then mark your new answer with a cross ☒.

8 What is the **main** purpose of this letter?

A	☒	To persuade you to join the club.
B	☒	To make you visit your doctor.
C	☒	To inform you of the activities at the club.
D	☐	To give you advice before your first visit.

> This is incorrect because Text B is a letter sent to new recruits so they have already joined.

> This is incorrect because only those 'not used to playing sport' are advised to visit their doctor.

> This is incorrect because no information about the activities is given.

(Total for Question 8 = 1 mark)

Answer question 9 with a cross in the two boxes ☒ you think are correct. If you change your mind about an answer, put a line through the box ☒ and then mark your new answer with a cross ☒.

9 Identify **two** features from the list below that show that Text B is a letter.

A	☒	bullet points
B	☐	use of Yours sincerely
C	☒	heading
D	☐	address and date
E	☒	contact number
F	☒	logo

> Even though these features are all in Text B, they are incorrect answers because they do not show it is a letter.

(Total for Question 9 = 2 marks)

10 Identify **two** things you are told in Text B you must do **before** you take part in activities with The Silly Army?

You do **not** need to write in sentences.

1. notify them of any medication

2. sense of fun

> 1 is incorrect because Text B says you must let helpers know of any medical conditions, not medication. The question asks for 'two things you are told in Text B you must do', so answer 2 is also incorrect because a 'sense of fun' is not something you do.

(Total for Question 10 = 2 marks)

11 Your friend wants to come to The Silly Army with you, but is a little worried about health and safety.

Using Text B give **two** reasons to reassure your friend that The Silly Army takes health and safety seriously.

You do **not** need to write in sentences.

1 wear a helmet

2 you will be safe when getting fit

> 1 is incorrect because it is an instruction not a reason – 'because helmets are provided' would be a reason. Answer 2 does not explain why you will be safe, which is what the question is asking.

(Total for Question 11 = 2 marks)

12 According to Text B, how should you contact The Silly Army if you have a question?

You do **not** need to write in sentences.

Speak to the Silly Army leader

> This is incorrect because it does not explain *how* you should contact him, i.e. by telephone.

(Total for Question 12 = 1 mark)

13 You want some friends to come along to The Silly Army, so you send a group email.

Using the information from Text B, what **two** points about The Silly Army would you include in your email?

You do **not** need to write in sentences.

1 go to the website

2 it is free of charge

> 1 is incorrect because it is not a point about the Silly Army. Answer 2 is incorrect because the information is from Text A not Text B.

(Total for Question 13 = 2 marks)

TOTAL FOR SECTION B = 10 MARKS
TOTAL FOR PAPER = 20 MARKS

Sample Writing answers – pass

Writing Level 1 pass answer

There are **two** tasks which assess your writing skills.

Remember that spelling, punctuation and grammar will be assessed in **both** tasks.

Task 1

Information

You are a member of a group trying to raise money for your local hospital. You receive the email below from one of your group.

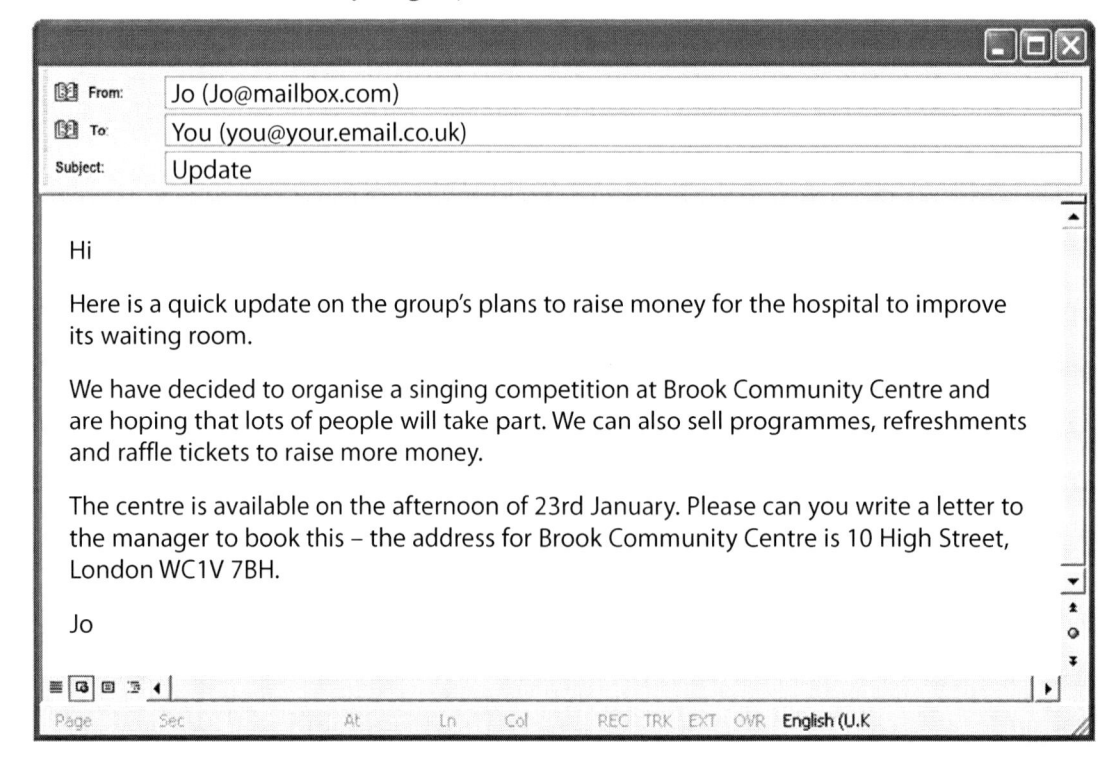

From: Jo (Jo@mailbox.com)
To: You (you@your.email.co.uk)
Subject: Update

Hi

Here is a quick update on the group's plans to raise money for the hospital to improve its waiting room.

We have decided to organise a singing competition at Brook Community Centre and are hoping that lots of people will take part. We can also sell programmes, refreshments and raffle tickets to raise more money.

The centre is available on the afternoon of 23rd January. Please can you write a letter to the manager to book this – the address for Brook Community Centre is 10 High Street, London WC1V 7BH.

Jo

Writing Task

Write a letter to Jill Smith, the manager of Brook Community Centre, to book the centre for the singing competition.

In your letter you should:

- introduce yourself and the reason for raising money
- ask to book the centre
- explain how you want to use the centre.

Remember to set your letter out correctly.

(15)

Begin your letter on the next page.

> Holyhead School
> Milestone Lane
> Holyhead Road
> Handsworth
> Birmingham
> B21 04N
>
> Thursday 27th May, 2010

Ms Jill Smith

Brook Community Centre

10 High Street

London

WC1V 7BH

Dear Ms Smith,

My name is Nawaal Farah. I am writing to you because I would like to book, Brook Community Centre on the afternoon of the 23rd of January. I would like to use your hall because I want to raise money to improve the hospital's waiting room.

I would like to book your community centre to put on a activity how we can raise money for the hospitals waiting room. The activity I would like is an singing competition. This is a great idea because people can have fun singing and the money they give us will improve the waiting room for the hospital which they wouldn't think they will spend it on something useless.

I would like to maybe use the whole hall and put on a stage. The people at the back may not see it so a TV as well. I want a table which they will be lots of drink and food.

Yours sincerely

A: Form, communication and purpose = 7 marks
B: Spelling, punctuation and grammar = 5 marks
Total = 12/15

(TOTAL FOR TASK 1 = 15 MARKS)

Assessment

What has been done well	
Communicates the main details successfully	Asks to book the centre on the given date and explains why.
Uses appropriate tone	Polite, no slang.
Correct letter format	Two addresses set out correctly, date, appropriate greeting and matching close.
Some attempt to structure	Uses paragraphs for different sections of the letter.
Reasonable technical accuracy	Accurate spelling.
	Generally accurate use of full stops, some correct use of apostrophes.
	Accurate subject-verb agreement, use of tenses.
What could be improved	
Clearer explanation of detailed requirements	E.g. position of stage and table.
Clearer expression of ideas	E.g. at the end of paragraph 2, the meaning of 'which they wouldn't think they will spend it on something useless' is unclear. The final sentence of paragraph 3 should be 'I want a table **on** which **there** will be lots of drink and food.'
Add conclusion requesting confirmation of booking	In case the date requested is no longer available.
Organisation of ideas	There is some repetition of ideas, e.g. beginning of paragraph 2.
Vary the sentence structure	Several sentences begin with, or include, the phrase 'I would like'.
Correct use of a/an	Use 'an' before words beginning with a vowel, e.g. 'activity', but 'a' before words beginning with a consonant, e.g. 'singing'.

Task 2

Information

You recently used the website below to buy a pair of these trainers.

ShoeWorld.co.uk

High Top Fashion Trainers

£36.99

☆☆☆☆☆

(23 customer reviews)

Write a Review

Colour: **Black**

Code: **111777777**

Product information

Black High Top Trainers. Canvas upper with white laces and white rubber sole and toe, man-made inner.

Writing Task

You have only worn your trainers a few times and they are now falling apart.

Write an email to the company to complain.

You may wish to include:

- how long you have had the trainers
- what the fault is
- what you want them to do about it.

(10)

Begin your answer on the next page.

Assessment

New Message

From: you@your.email.co.uk
To: CustomerServices@ShoeWorld.co.uk
Subject: Complaint

Dear Customer Services,

My name is Shaleen Baker and I am writing this letter to explain to you the fault with my Black High Top Fashion Trainers I bought three week ago.

I've had these High Top Fashion Trainers for three weeks now and they seem to be falling apart every time I wear them.

The fault I have with these trainers are that they keep falling apart every time I wear them and also the colour is fading away.

If it is no trouble I would like you to send me my £36.99p back if you cannot find a better and suitable replacement for the Black High Top Fashion Trainers.

Yours sincerly
Shaleen Baker

A: Form, communication and purpose = 4 marks
B: Spelling, punctuation and grammar = 4 marks
Total – 8/10

(TOTAL FOR TASK 2 = 10 MARKS)

TOTAL FOR PAPER = 25 MARKS

What has been done well	
Includes most relevant details	E.g. make, colour, cost, description of fault, action to be taken.
Polite, business-like tone	Formal vocabulary, no use of slang.
Correct format	Appropriate greeting and matching close for a formal email.
Good level of technical accuracy	One spelling mistake, accurate use of full stops, few grammatical errors. |//
What could be improved	
Repetiton of information	No need to repeat full name of trainers each time; description of fault repeated.
Link related information together	E.g. paragraphs 2 and 3 could be combined.
Use capital letters only where necessary	'black' is not part of the name of the trainers.
Check subject-verb agreement	'The **fault** … **is** that they keep falling apart'.
Correct spelling	'sincer**e**ly'.

Sample Writing answers – fail

Writing Level 1 fail answer

There are **two** tasks which assess your writing skills.

Remember that spelling, punctuation and grammar will be assessed in **both** tasks.

Task 1

Information

You are a member of a group trying to raise money for your local hospital. You receive the email below from one of your group.

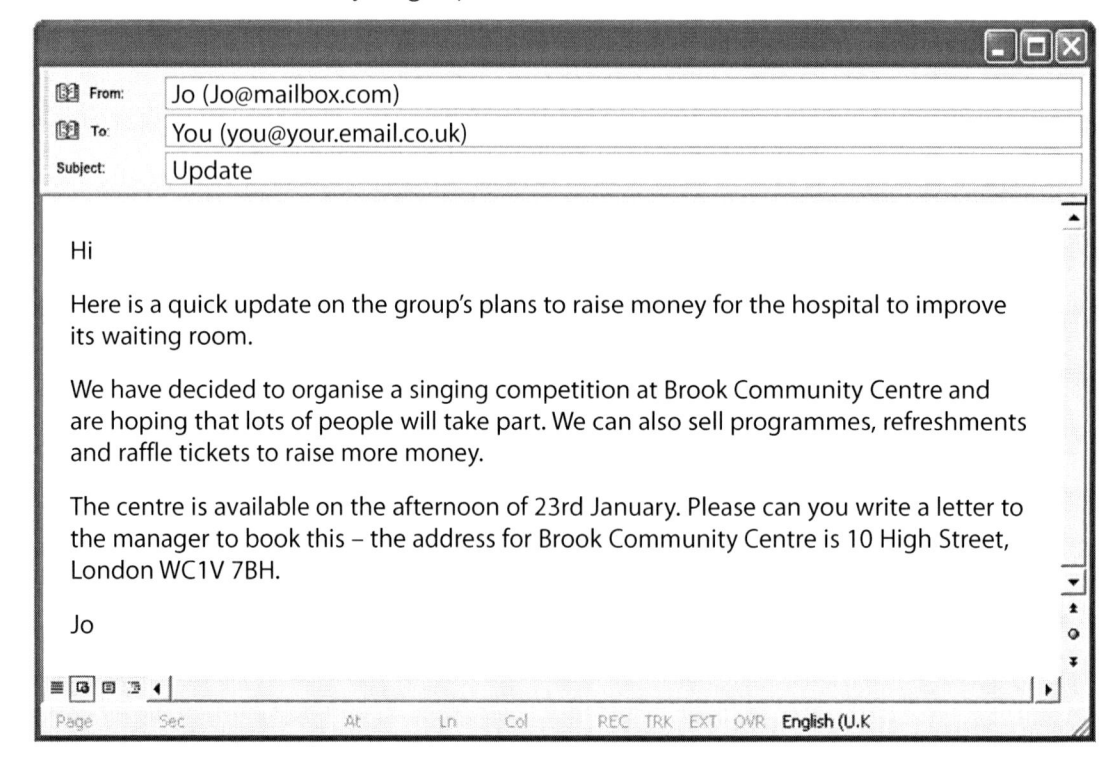

From: Jo (Jo@mailbox.com)
To: You (you@your.email.co.uk)
Subject: Update

Hi

Here is a quick update on the group's plans to raise money for the hospital to improve its waiting room.

We have decided to organise a singing competition at Brook Community Centre and are hoping that lots of people will take part. We can also sell programmes, refreshments and raffle tickets to raise more money.

The centre is available on the afternoon of 23rd January. Please can you write a letter to the manager to book this – the address for Brook Community Centre is 10 High Street, London WC1V 7BH.

Jo

Writing Task

Write a letter to Jill Smith, the manager of Brook Community Centre, to book the centre for the singing competition.

In your letter you should:

- introduce yourself and the reason for raising money
- ask to book the centre
- explain how you want to use the centre.

Remember to set your letter out correctly.

(15)

Begin your letter on the next page.

Holyhead Road
Handsworth
Birmingham
B21 0HN

10 High Street
London
WC1V 7BH

Dear Jill Smith

Hi My name is Rajwinder. I am writing to you because I wanted to Book the centre for the singing competion, I am raising this money because I wanted to improve the hospital wating room.

I want to use the center, a row of chears and a stage with a microphone.

Your sincile Rajwinder

A: Form, communication and purpose = 2 marks
B: Spelling, punctuation and grammar = 3 marks
Total – 5/15

(TOTAL FOR TASK 1 = 15 MARKS)

Assessment

What has been done well	
Communicates some information	Wants to book the centre for a singing competition, purpose of raising funds, additional requests.
Includes some features of correct layout	Two addresses in correct position, greeting and matching close.
What could be improved	
Include all essential information	Especially the date when the centre is wanted!
Include more background information	E.g. what organisation is involved, numbers expected, more details about the fund-raising event.
Include name and organisation of person who should receive the letter	In case the letter is misplaced after being opened.
Date the letter	Letters may be filed according to their date and you can use the date as a reference point if you need to write a follow-up letter.
Use appropriate tone consistently	'Hi' is not appropriate in a formal letter.
Separate sentences accurately	In the first paragraph, 'I am raising this money …' should begin a new sentence.
Correct some spellings	E.g writeing (should be 'writing'), competion (competition), wating (waiting), chears (chairs), sincile (sincerely). Also, the American spelling 'center' is used as well as the UK English 'centre'.
Use correct tense of verb	'I am writing because I **want** …'; 'I am raising this money because I **want** …' (instead of 'wanted').
Avoid use of unnecessary capital letters	E.g. 'Book' does not begin a sentence and is not a name.

Task 2

Information

You recently used the website below to buy a pair of these trainers.

ShoeWorld.co.uk

High Top Fashion Trainers

£36.99

★★★★★

(23 customer reviews)

Write a Review

Colour: **Black**

Code: **111777777**

Product information

Black High Top Trainers. Canvas upper with white laces and white rubber sole and toe, man-made inner.

Writing Task

You have only worn your trainers a few times and they are now falling apart.

Write an email to the company to complain.

You may wish to include:

- how long you have had the trainers
- what the fault is
- what you want them to do about it.

(10)

Begin your answer on the next page.

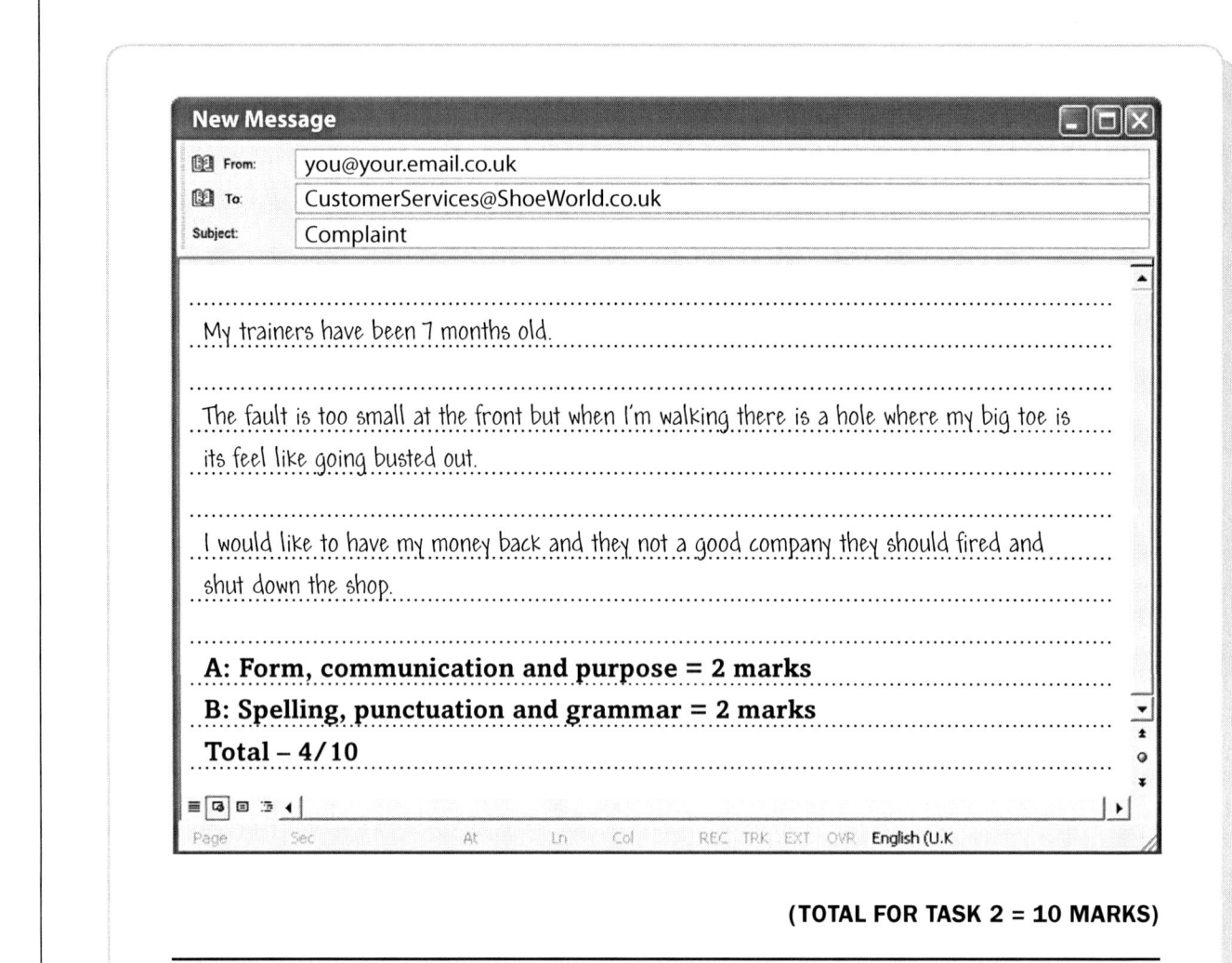

Assessment

New Message

From: you@your.email.co.uk
To: CustomerServices@ShoeWorld.co.uk
Subject: Complaint

My trainers have been 7 months old.

The fault is too small at the front but when I'm walking there is a hole where my big toe is its feel like going busted out.

I would like to have my money back and they not a good company they should fired and shut down the shop.

A: Form, communication and purpose = 2 marks
B: Spelling, punctuation and grammar = 2 marks
Total – 4/10

(TOTAL FOR TASK 2 = 10 MARKS)

TOTAL FOR PAPER = 25 MARKS

What has been done well	
Gives some relevant information	E.g. how long since bought, some description of fault, action to be taken.
Reasonable technical accuracy	Accurate spelling and punctuation.
What could be improved	
Include more detail	E.g. the make of the trainers, date bought.
Express ideas more clearly	E.g. what is meant by 'the fault is too small at the front' and 'its feel like going busted out'?; who is meant by 'they' in the final sentence?
Use correct format for an email	Include an appropriate greeting and close, including signing off with own name.
Separate sentences correctly	Begin a new sentence after '… where my big toe is' and after '… not a good company'.
Check that sentences are complete	There is a word missing from 'they not good company' and 'they should fired'.
Use correct tense of verb	'My trainers **are** 7 months old.'

Reading Level 1 practice assessment

SECTION A

Read Text A and answer questions 1 – 7.

Text A

You have to do work experience as part of your school curriculum. You are given this information sheet by your work experience adviser.

WORK EXPERIENCE – WHAT YOU NEED TO KNOW

Work experience is an opportunity to help you prepare for your future.
It gives you a chance to:
- practice and develop skills necessary in the workplace
- work with people who are experts in their field
- learn more about the world of work
- gain experience of a working environment.

HOW DO I PREPARE FOR WORK EXPERIENCE?

As your placement approaches your teacher will provide a work experience preparation session. It will cover health and safety in the workplace, going for interview, dress code, and how to plan your journey, etc.

DO I HAVE TO WORK THE WHOLE DAY?

This will depend on the job you do for placement. You will be expected to work the same sort of hours as the business you are in. For example if you work in an office you will usually work 9am to 5pm, but if you work in construction you will usually have a much earlier start. Whatever you do there is a maximum of an 8 hour day (not including breaks).

WHAT TIPS CAN YOU GIVE ME FOR A GOOD PLACEMENT?
- Be on time.
- Wear appropriate dress – follow dress codes and use protective clothing if needed.
- Follow instructions especially health and safety rules.
- Ask for help when you need it.
- Be enthusiastic and take pride in your work!

Content provided courtesy of Oxfordshire Education Business Partnership (www.oebp.org.uk)

Answer questions 1 to 3 with a cross in the box ☒. If you change your mind about an answer, put a line through the box ☒ and then mark your new answer with a cross ☒.

1   The **main** purpose of this information sheet is to:

A	☐	explain some important features of work experience
B	☐	persuade you to apply for work experience
C	☐	describe different types of work experience
D	☐	advise you how to find a work experience placement

(Total for Question 1 = 1 mark)

2   According to Text A, **one** benefit of work experience is that:

A	☐	you will meet new people
B	☐	you can find out what working life is like
C	☐	you can wear whatever you like
D	☐	you will get a job for the future

(Total for Question 2 = 1 mark)

3   Which of these statements about work experience is true?

A	☐	You will always start work at 9 a.m.
B	☐	You must work the same hours as everyone else.
C	☐	You must not work more than 8 hours per day.
D	☐	You will not be allowed any breaks.

(Total for Question 3 = 1 mark)

4   Name **one** action you should take to get ready for your work experience.

....

(Total for Question 4 = 1 mark)

5 List **two** ways that Text A is presented to help the reader find information.

You do **not** need to write in sentences.

1 ....

2 ....

(Total for Question 5 = 2 marks)

6 List **two** important pieces of advice from Text A that you would suggest to someone wanting to get the most out of a work experience placement.

You do **not** need to write in sentences.

1 ....

....

2 ....

....

(Total for Question 6 = 2 marks)

7 You have been invited to an interview for a work experience placement. What important details about your placement should you aim to find out during the interview?

Give **two** suggestions using the information from Text A.

You do **not** need to write in sentences.

1 ....

....

2 ....

....

(Total for Question 7 = 2 marks)

TOTAL FOR SECTION A = 10 MARKS

SECTION B

Read Text B and answer questions 8 – 13.

Text B

During your research on work experience, you have found this web page.

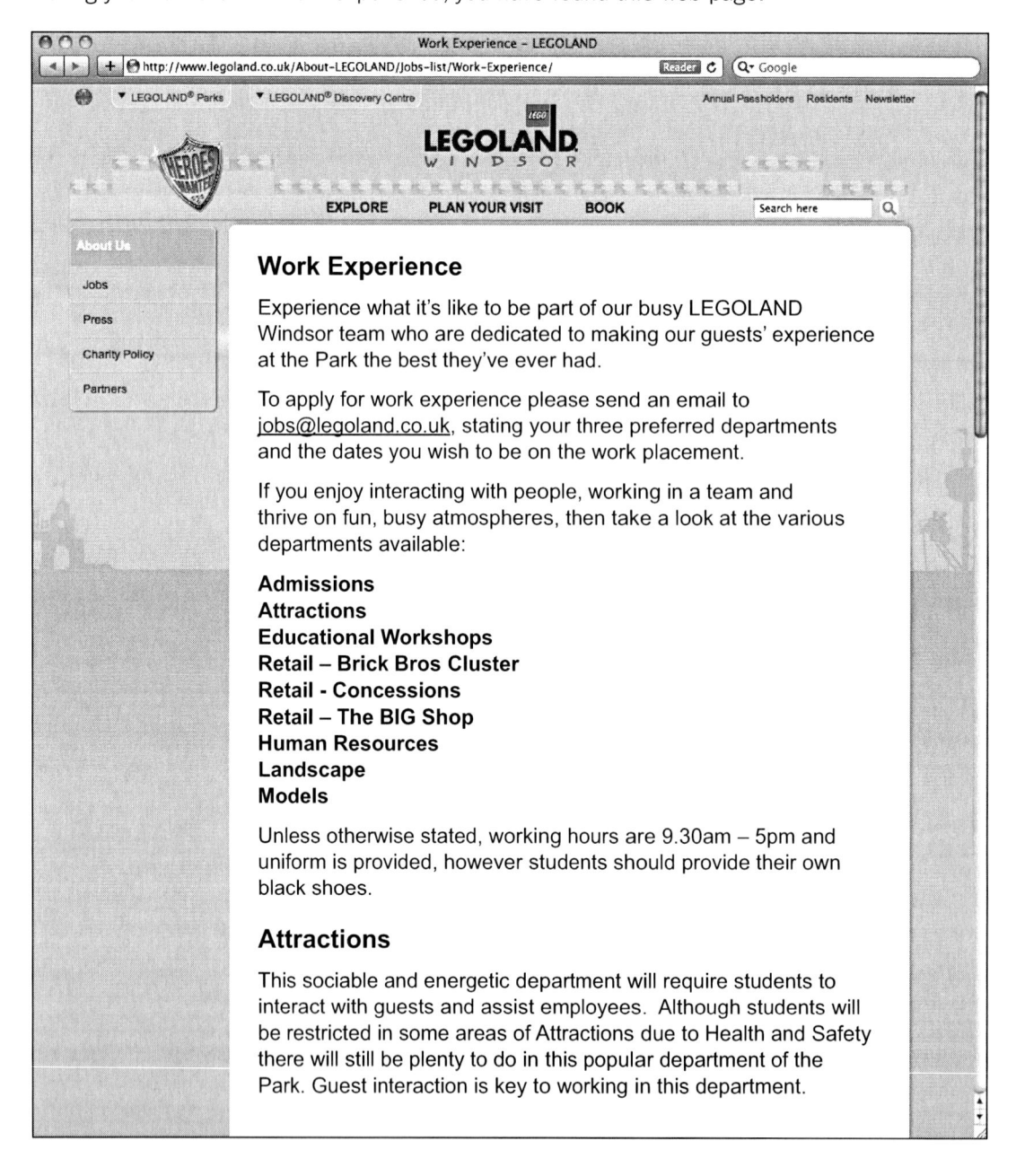

Work Experience – LEGOLAND

http://www.legoland.co.uk/About-LEGOLAND/Jobs-list/Work-Experience/

LEGOLAND® Parks | LEGOLAND® Discovery Centre | Annual Passholders Residents Newsletter

LEGOLAND WINDSOR

EXPLORE   PLAN YOUR VISIT   BOOK   Search here

About Us
Jobs
Press
Charity Policy
Partners

Work Experience

Experience what it's like to be part of our busy LEGOLAND Windsor team who are dedicated to making our guests' experience at the Park the best they've ever had.

To apply for work experience please send an email to jobs@legoland.co.uk, stating your three preferred departments and the dates you wish to be on the work placement.

If you enjoy interacting with people, working in a team and thrive on fun, busy atmospheres, then take a look at the various departments available:

Admissions
Attractions
Educational Workshops
Retail – Brick Bros Cluster
Retail - Concessions
Retail – The BIG Shop
Human Resources
Landscape
Models

Unless otherwise stated, working hours are 9.30am – 5pm and uniform is provided, however students should provide their own black shoes.

Attractions

This sociable and energetic department will require students to interact with guests and assist employees. Although students will be restricted in some areas of Attractions due to Health and Safety there will still be plenty to do in this popular department of the Park. Guest interaction is key to working in this department.

Answer question 8 with a cross in the box you think is correct ☒. If you change your mind about an answer, put a line through the box ☒ and then mark your new answer with a cross ☒.

8   What is the **main** purpose of this web page?

A	☐	To inform you of the hours you will work.
B	☐	To describe the different theme park attractions.
C	☐	To persuade you to apply for a placement.
D	☐	To advise you about Health and Safety restrictions.

(Total for Question 8 = 1 mark)

Answer question 9 with a cross in the two boxes ☒ you think are correct. If you change your mind about an answer, put a line through the box ☒ and then mark your new answer with a cross ☒.

9   Identify **two** features from the list below that show that Text B is a web page.

A	☐	bullet points
B	☐	email address
C	☐	heading
D	☐	menu bar
E	☐	tabs
F	☐	bold text

(Total for Question 9 = 2 marks)

10 Identify **two** things you must include in your email application.

You do **not** need to write in sentences.

1 ....

....

2 ....

....

(Total for Question 10 = 2 marks)

11 What type of person would be suitable to work in the Attractions Department at Legoland?

Give **two** suggestions using the information from Text B.

You do **not** need to write in sentences.

1 ....

2 ....

(Total for Question 11 = 2 marks)

12 According to Text B, what do students on work experience need to provide themselves?

You do **not** need to write in sentences.

....

(Total for Question 12 = 1 mark)

13 You have a friend looking for work experience in the Windsor area.

What **two** points from Text B would you use to recommend Legoland to your friend?

You do **not** need to write in sentences.

1 ....

....

2 ....

....

(Total for Question 13 = 2 marks)

TOTAL FOR SECTION B = 10 MARKS
TOTAL FOR PAPER = 20 MARKS

Mark scheme: Reading

Reading Level 1 practice assessment answers

Section A

Question Number	Answer	Mark
1	A – explain some important features of work experience	(1)

Question Number	Answer	Mark
2	B – you can find out what working life is like	(1)

Question Number	Answer	Mark
3	C – You must not work more than 8 hours per day.	(1)

Question Number	Answer	Mark
4	• attend a work experience preparation session (1) One mark for a correct answer, up to a maximum of **one** mark.	(1)

Question Number	Answer	Mark
5	Answers may include: • Sub-headings in bold/capital letters to highlight (1) • Questions to organise information into sections (1) • Bullet points to list related information (1) One mark for each correct answer, up to a maximum of **two** marks.	(2)

Question Number	Answer	Mark
6	Answers may include: • be on time (1) • wear appropriate dress (1) • follow instructions (1) • ask for help if needed (1) • be enthusiastic/take pride in work (1) Accept any reasonable answer, based on the text, up to a maximum of **two** marks.	(2)

Question Number	Answer	Mark
7	Answers may include: • location of the business to plan the journey (1) • type of work involved (1) • hours of work (1) • health and safety rules (1) • dress code/any protective clothing needed (1) Accept any reasonable answer, based on the text, up to a maximum of **two** marks.	(2)

Section B

Question Number	Answer	Mark
8	C – To persuade you to apply for a placement.	(1)

Question Number	Answer	Mark
9	D – menu bar E – tabs One mark for each correct answer.	(2)

Question Number	Answer	Mark
10	Your three preferred departments (1) Dates you wish to be on placement (1) One mark for each correct answer.	(2)

Question Number	Answer	Mark
11	Answers may include: • sociable/enjoy interacting with people (1) • helpful (1) • team players (1) • energetic/thrive on busy departments (1) Accept any reasonable answer, based on the text, up to a maximum of **two** marks.	(2)

Question Number	Answer	Mark
12	A pair of black shoes.	(1)

Question Number	Answer	Mark
13	Answers may include: • an exciting, fun place to work (1) • could lead to a permanent job (1) • many different departments/variety of jobs (1) • can apply by email (1) • uniform provided (1) Accept any reasonable answer, based on the text, up to a maximum of **two** marks.	(2)

Practice assessments

Mapping to Functional Skills Criteria for English Level 1

Reading

Question	Fixed marks	Open marks	Mapping to standard — Read and understand a range of straightforward texts			
			(L1.2.1) Identify the main points and ideas and how they are presented in a variety of texts	(L1.2.2) Read and understand texts in detail	(L1.2.3) Utilise information contained in texts	(L1.2.4) Identify suitable responses to texts
1	1		✓			
2	1			✓		
3	1			✓		
4	1			✓		
5		2	✓			
6		2			✓	
7		2			✓	
8	1		✓			
9	2		✓			
10	2			✓		
11		2				✓
12	1				✓	
13		2				✓
Total marks:			6	5	5	4
Total percentage:			30	25	25	20

© Pearson Education Limited 2010

Speaking, listening and communication Level 1 practice assessment

Informal discussion

Your school or college has links with a similar organisation in another country. Your class is going to host a group of students from this school or college for a week. You have been asked to discuss places of interest for this group to visit to get the best impression of your area.

In pairs or small groups of up to five, discuss ideas for places you could take your guests.

Before the discussion, try to imagine what would interest a foreign visitor of your age to your area. Which of your own favourite places would be most suitable? Some ideas to get you started are given below.

- What is my area most famous for? What places attract most visitors and what do these places show about the general area?

- What attractions do I like myself? How much are they likely to cost and how easy are they to get to?

- What is the purpose of the visit to your area (e.g. part of a course, a holiday, a mixture of both)? What would a visitor from another country most want to see and do on a short break? Would all visitors enjoy the same kind of activity?

- Your visitors might have a different culture and/or different language. How could you deal with this, and what opportunities might this offer?

- Would you need to take any steps to look after the health and safety of your visitors?

Formal discussion

Your school or college is considering whether to change the start and end times and the length of the school day. The Head Teacher/Principal and the Board of Governors have asked for the views of all parties concerned, including teachers, parents and students. Each class has been asked to put forward their recommendations with reasons for their views.

In a group of up to five, discuss and try to agree what changes your group would recommend to be made to the school day. Give reasons to support your views.

Before the discussion, write down your own ideas on the subject. Do some research to find information to support your views. Some ideas to get you started are given below.

> Are there any government regulations on when and how long we have to be at school/college?
>
> When do other schools/colleges in the local area and elsewhere start and end their day? What reasons do they give for this?
>
> If we started earlier, we could finish earlier and I'd still have leisure time after doing my homework. I work better in the mornings anyway. In winter we would get home before it gets dark.
>
> If we started later I wouldn't feel so tired in the morning, so I'd work better. There'd be fewer cars on the road during the rush hour – but what if your parents go to work earlier?
>
> If we had a longer school day, we would learn more and get better grades. We could have more time for lunch and lunchtime clubs.
>
> If we had a shorter school day, we wouldn't get so tired and we'd work better. There'd be more time for after-school activities.

Practice assessments

Functional Skills English Level 1: Speaking, Listening and Communication Assessment Record Sheet

Please complete the following information (use a separate sheet for each learner).

Learner name:	Learner number:	Centre number:

Activity: Formal	Date:
Please use the space below to note the context of the activity, how it was organised and any learner support.	

Activity: Informal	Date:
Please use the space below to note the context of the activity, how it was organised and any learner support.	

Level 1: Take full part in formal and informal discussions and exchanges that include unfamiliar subjects.

The grid should be applied on a 'best fit' basis. To achieve a Level 1 overall, a learner should have met each of the Level 1 standards at least once.

Just below Level 1	✓	Achieved Level 1	✓
Makes some relevant contributions to discussion		Makes relevant and extended contributions to discussions	
Sometimes allows for and responds to others' input		Allows for and responds to others' input	
Some preparation for the formal discussion of ideas and opinions		Preparation supports contribution to the formal discussion of ideas and opinions	
Makes some different kinds of contributions to discussions		Makes different kinds of contributions to discussions	
Some information/points of view presented clearly, with some use of appropriate language		Presents information/points of view clearly and in appropriate language	

Please tick the box if the learner has achieved Level 1:
Centre summative comment:
Assessor signature: Date:

108 © Pearson Education Limited 2010

Writing Level 1 practice assessment

There are **two** tasks which assess your writing skills. Task 1 is worth 15 marks and Task 2 is worth 10 marks.

Remember that spelling, punctuation and grammar will be assessed in **both** tasks.

You may use a dictionary.

Task 1

Information

Your school or college has asked you to write an article giving advice on revision for exams for the Student Forum page on its website.

To research your article, you have asked your friends and classmates and looked on the internet for revision tips. You have made the notes below from some of the information you have collected.

> 'I always make a revision timetable with the dates of all my exams. That way, I know which subjects to revise for and I can plan how long I've got to revise each one. I usually revise a different subject every day, but some people prefer to break it up by doing a bit each day on lots of subjects.' **Jenny**

> 'It's tempting to put off revising the subjects, or parts of subjects, you find hard, but I try to tackle them first when I'm feeling fresh and can concentrate better. Don't do too much at once though – give yourself some time to relax.' **Robbie**

> 'I hate distractions when I'm revising. I like to be on my own where it's quiet – I even turn off my mobile! I need plenty of space too so I can spread things out – I hate it when I have to spend ages looking for the book I need.' **Rajinder**

> 'My sister records all her notes on a dictaphone and listens to it as she's walking round the house doing other stuff. I learn better when I can see what I'm learning, so I make revision cards and write little notes with important words and phrases on – then I stick them on doors and walls and furniture so I see them all the time as a reminder.' **Ibrahim**

> 'If I start feeling stressed, I go for a walk. Somebody told me exercise improves your memory too!' **Alex**

> 'Get friends and family to test you...' www.revisioncentre.co.uk

> 'Eat well, and eat healthy foods.' www.educationforum.co.uk

Writing task

Write an article giving revision tips suitable for your school or college website. Give your article a suitable title.

In your article, you may wish to:
- describe a range of ways of revising for exams
- explain how they might be helpful
- suggest those you think are most effective.

TOTAL FOR TASK 1 = 15 MARKS

Task 2

Information

You have been asked to be in charge of sending out the invitations to a family celebration. You need to include directions on how to get to the party venue.

Writing task

Write clear, detailed directions to your guests, telling them how to reach the venue for the party.

In your directions, you may wish to consider:
- how the guests will be travelling
- how familiar they are with the area
- how to present your directions.

TOTAL FOR TASK 2 = 10 MARKS
TOTAL FOR PAPER = 25 MARKS

Mark scheme: Writing

Writing Level 1 practice assessment marking

Marks for each task are awarded by applying the two grids below:
A: Form, communication and purpose
B: Spelling, punctuation and grammar.

Each marking grid, A and B, should be applied independently because you may have a different level of ability under each heading.

Task		
1	Write an article giving revision tips suitable for your school or college website. Give your article a suitable title. In your article, you may wish to: • describe a range of ways of revising for exams • explain how they might be helpful • suggest those you think are most effective. **(15 marks)**	
	Indicative content	
	• Uses relevant organisational features of an article. • Uses appropriate tone/language when writing the article. • Uses some detail when describing and explaining the revision tips.	

Mark	A: Form, communication and purpose
0	No rewardable material.
1–3	• Communicates relevant information and ideas at a basic level. • Presents information with limited sequencing of ideas. • Uses language, format and structure for specific audience and purpose to a limited extent. • Makes limited use of appropriate conventions for writing an article.
4–6	• Communicates relevant information and ideas with some success. • Presents information with some logical sequencing of ideas, although this is not sustained throughout the response. • Uses language, format and structure for specific audience and purpose for some of the response. • Makes some use of appropriate conventions for writing an article.
7–9	• Communicates relevant information and ideas successfully, although there may be minor lapses. • Presents information with logical sequencing of ideas and this is evident for the majority of the response. • Uses language, format and structure for specific audience and purpose throughout the response, although there may be occasional slips/omissions. • Makes use consistently of appropriate conventions for writing an article. Any omissions do not detract from the overall quality of the response.

Mark	B: Spelling, punctuation and grammar
0	No rewardable material.
1–2	• There is limited use of correct grammar, and consistent use of tense is minimal. • Spelling and punctuation are used with limited accuracy and errors will often affect clarity of meaning.
3–4	• There is some correct use of grammar and some correct use of tense, although not sustained throughout the response. • Spelling and punctuation are used with some accuracy, although errors will sometimes affect clarity of meaning.
5–6	• There is correct use of grammar and consistent use of tense throughout the response, although there may be occasional errors. • Spelling and punctuation are used with general accuracy and meaning is clearly conveyed, with only occasional lapses.

Task	
2	Write clear, detailed directions to your guests telling them how to reach the venue for the party. In your directions, you may wish to consider: • how the guests will be travelling • how familiar they are with the area • how to present your directions. **(10 marks)**
	Indicative content • Uses relevant organisational features. • Uses relevant tone/language when writing directions. • Shows awareness of audience.

Mark	A: Form, communication and purpose
0	No rewardable material.
1–2	• Communicates relevant information and ideas at a basic level. • Presents information with limited sequencing of ideas. • Uses language, format and structure for specific audience and purpose to a limited extent. • Response has limited level of appropriate detail.
3–4	• Communicates relevant information and ideas with some success. • Presents information with some logical sequencing of ideas, although this is not sustained throughout the response. • Uses language, format and structure for specific audience and purpose for some of the response. • Response has some level of appropriate detail.
5–6	• Communicates relevant information and ideas successfully, although there may be minor lapses. • Presents information with logical sequencing of ideas and this is evident for the majority of the response. • Uses language, format and structure for specific audience and purpose throughout the response, although there may be occasional slips/omissions. • Response has developed level of appropriate detail.

Mark	B: Spelling, punctuation and grammar
0	No rewardable material.
1–2	• There is some use of correct grammar and some appropriate use of tense. • Spelling and punctuation are used with limited accuracy and errors will sometimes affect clarity of meaning.
3–4	• There is mostly correct use of grammar and mostly consistent use of tense throughout the response, although there may be occasional errors. • Spelling and punctuation are used mostly with accuracy, with some lapses.

Mapping to Functional Skills Criteria for English Level 1

Writing

Skill standard

Write a range of texts to communicate information, ideas and opinions, using formats and styles suitable for their purpose and audience.

Question	Skill standard description	No. of marks	%
Q1 Q2	(L1.3.1) Write clearly and coherently, including an appropriate level of detail.	15	60
Q1 Q2	(L1.3.2) Present information in a logical sequence.		
Q1 Q2	(L1.3.3) Use language, format and structure suitable for purpose and audience.		
Q1 Q2	(L1.3.4) Use correct grammar, including correct and consistent use of tense.	10	40
Q1 Q2	(L1.3.5) Ensure written work includes generally accurate punctuation and spelling, and that meaning is clear.		
	Total for Writing	25	100